Dating Twentieth Century Photographs

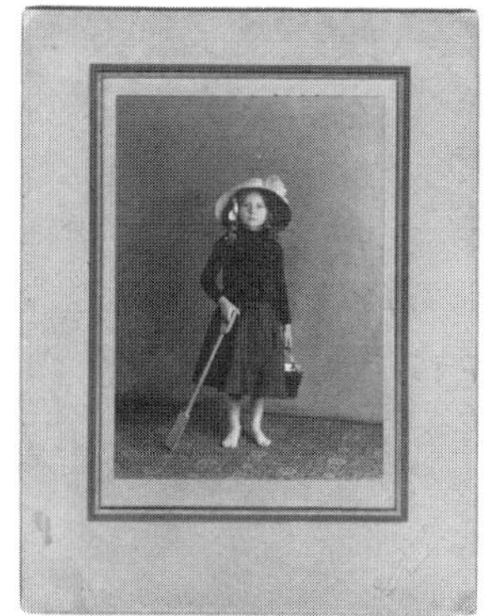

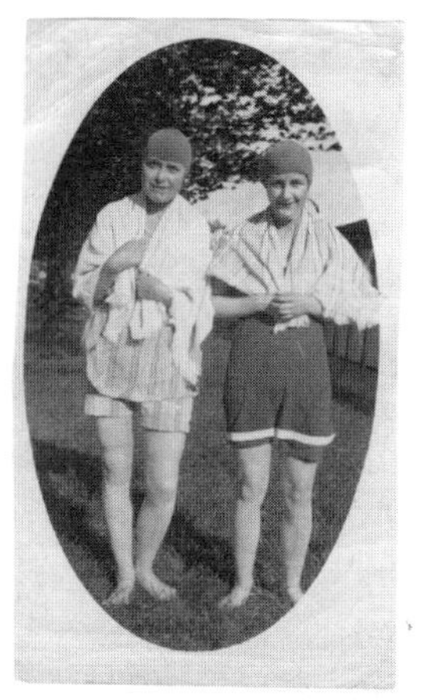

ROBERT POLS

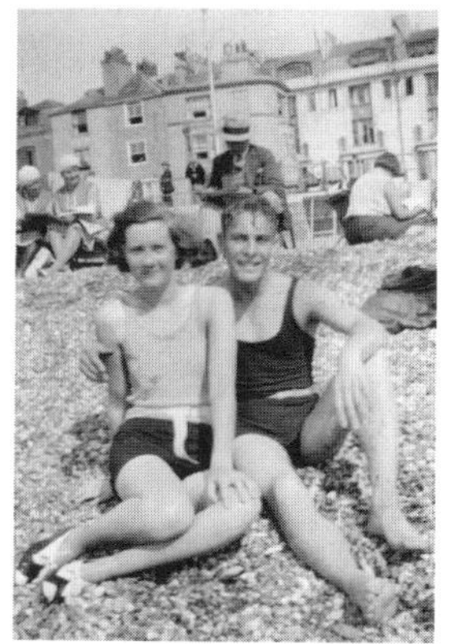

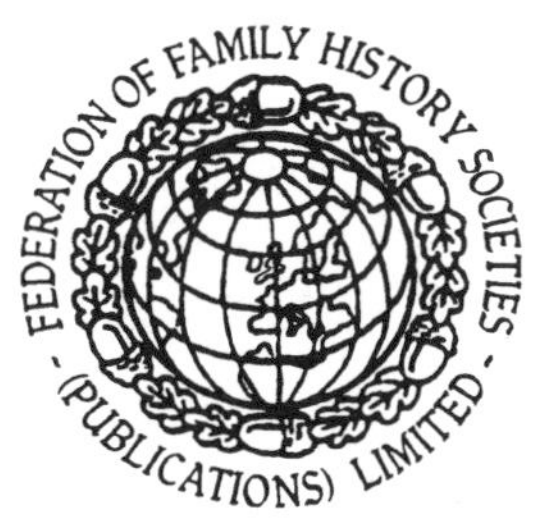

Published by
The Fedration of Family History Societies (Publications) Ltd
Units 15-16, Chesham Industrial Estate
Oram Street, Bury
Lancashire BL9 6EN

© Robert Pols

ISBN: 1 86006 191 5

First Published 2005

This book and its companion
Dating Nineteenth Century Photographs
replaces the previous publication
Dating Old Photographs

Printed and bound at The Alden Press
Osney Mead, Oxford OX1 0EF

Contents

Introduction

Writing in 1900, Frank Meadow Sutcliffe looked back on the tribulations of the 19th century photographer. "The weight of the camera and its six dark slides often felt like the last straw on my back. I used to fill the slides with plates and go out into the country in search of the picturesque, but before I had got clear of the town I had forgotten my quest altogether, for the camera began to get so heavy that . . . my thoughts were entirely confined to the burden on my back, and the weights I carried in either hand."

But photography was about to become much less arduous. In the year those words were written, the Box Brownie was launched, and that simple little camera was to change the world of imaging beyond recognition. Photography became something that just about everyone could try.

Despite having been easy to take, however, 20th century photographs are not always easy to date. The vast majority of family pictures from the Victorian era were taken in a studio, where backcloths, props and furniture often gave valuable pointers towards one decade or another. Cartes de visite and cabinet prints, the standard contents of the Victorian album, were pasted to cardboard mounts, and changing fashions of mount design provide very useful help with dating. But cartes and cabinet prints survived for only a few years of the new century, and a convenient battery of clues disappeared with them. Studio pictures did not disappear, but they no longer dominated the photographic scene. More and more people took their own photos and, because they needed enough light for the adequate exposure of their film, they took them out of doors. Some of their outdoor settings can be placed in time, but the majority are uninformative. A stretch of beach or an expanse of grass generally yields up less indication of date than a painted backcloth or a studio balustrade. Fortunately, the unhelpful landscape is likely to serve as a background to human beings, and human beings tend to be resolutely of their time.

Inevitably, therefore, the evidence of costume has to be leaned on rather heavily. That, in fact, is nothing new. Costume also gives great help in dating Victorian photographs. But it is often just one of several dating aids that can be used to place a 19th century photograph. In the case of 20th century photographs, it may be harder to accumulate a number of clues that corroborate each other.

Nevertheless, there are messages to be read. Professional photography still made a contribution to the family album, and there were broad trends in the taking and presentation of studio portraits. Elsewhere, people often chose to be pictured next to a proudly possessed (and datable) car, bicycle or motorcycle. Image size may also prove revealing if it relates to the size of the original negative — though the water can be muddied by the increasing ease with which enlargements were made. The information gained from such clues may often be no more precise than an earliest possible date, but two or three such details will often combine to allow a reasonably helpful conclusion.

This is fortunate, because the family historian's need to date photographs does not stop at the end of Victoria's reign, and the old pictures that people puzzle over often prove to be of 20th century origin. The most basic reason for dating still applies: we want the information because, quite simply, it *is* information. We are keen to know everything we can about those pieces of the past that have been handed down to us.

Attempts at dating may also have a specific agenda. We do not always know who the subjects of old portraits are, and by assigning them to an approximate period in time we can generally narrow down the possibilities. A sitter who was still young in one decade can hardly be the ancestor who married twenty years before. So, by asking ourselves if a portrait was made before or after the First World War or whether a snap belongs to the 1920s or 1930s, we feel our way towards a possible identification.

In other instances, we know who is depicted but would like an idea of the subject's age. We want to know, say, whether the picture was taken before or after marriage, or before or after becoming a parent or grandparent. It is not always easy to determine somebody's age. It can be difficult enough in the present. If a person asks us to guess his or her age, we may be quite unsure of the correct answer (despite having a fair notion of the direction in which it would be politic to err). Such problems can be much greater when we are looking at an image from the past. Young people seem to have looked older much earlier. This is perhaps partly because, before the 1950s, they went straight from dressing as children to dressing as adults, without a period in which teenage fashions intervened. At any rate, an idea of when a picture was taken can help us to determine the age of someone whose birth date we know.

There is one final motive for dating, and that applies to more recent pictures. Because we may be no better than our ancestors at annotating the photographs we take, we sometimes find ourselves trying to establish just which holiday or which Christmas a snap relates to. Our own pictures, as well as those of our forebears, can sometimes become the objects of uncertainty when, spurred by conscience, we try to document the images of our lives.

So, for a variety of reasons, 20th century photographs may become the focus of attempts at dating, and the aim of this book is to provide some support to those attempts. Picking up the thread where its companion 19th century volume left off, it surveys technical developments, and considers dating from the point of view of both artefact and image. As in the previous work, a selection of illustrations and a series of dating charts complete the offering.

There remains one issue to be considered. How much of the 20th century may be reasonably held to qualify as 'old'? Some of us, after all, lived through more than half of it. But what for many people constitutes memory is, for a growing number of family researchers, history. Indeed, there does seem to be a tendency for history to become ever younger, and television programmes already invite us to look back fondly to the 1990s. (Nostalgia, it has been aptly said, is not what it used to be.) A line needs to be drawn between the old and the recent, but it is debatable where that line should be.

The sensible solution has, I think, to be a slightly wobbly line. A clear-cut watershed date would be convenient, but life is not always so obliging. The arrival of the Box Brownie really did change photography in a way that makes a useful division between centuries, but no such landmark divides the 20th century in two. In fact, a number of important advances in photography belong to the 1930s, but only made a significant popular impact ten years or more after the Second World War. Yet common sense demands that discussion should concentrate on the earlier part of the century, for that period presents most would-be daters with the most problems.

The closest attention, therefore, is given to the years up about 1950. But where it seems appropriate, later developments are touched on briefly. The result is less a cut-off point than a tailing-off point. It is hoped that some extra assistance is thereby given to those who are sorting out their own photographs and to those family historians who are less weighed down by the uncertain advantages of age.

Photography in the 20th Century

The arrival of the snapshot

Despite pioneering experiments with paper and metals, it was glass that, from the 1850s, was the material increasingly employed as host for the photographic chemicals which, exposed to light, allowed an image to be formed. But glass plates, and the glass negatives that they became, were both weighty and fragile. A lighter and more flexible film base was needed before truly liberating developments in photography could take place. Celluloid met the requirements. Though invented in 1861, it was not at first made in the clear, thin and supple sheets that were necessary for photographic use. But in 1888 John Carbutt of Philadelphia began to produce celluloid in such a form, and George Eastman was quick to recognise its possibilities as a film base.

Already, in the 19th century, Eastman was introducing photographic ideas that were to dominate the 20th. In 1885 he invented a form of gelatin-coated, paper-backed film, which could be used in a roll in a purpose-built box camera. In 1889 he launched the No. 1 Kodak. This camera took circular pictures, 2 inches (5.1 cm) in diameter, about a hundred to a roll. The film was sealed in the camera. Once it had been exposed, the customer simply returned the complete package to the Eastman factory, where the film was removed and processed. The company then returned the camera, reloaded and ready for use, together with the set of prints. Eastman's slogan, "You press the button and we do the rest", summed up the procedure perfectly. The camera was easy to use and quickly became popular.

By 1890 Eastman had seen the possibilities of celluloid and was using it to produce rolls capable of giving 12 or 24 prints. (This may seem ungenerous when compared to the 100 pictures of earlier rolls, but it actually responded to the user's anxiety to see the results.) In 1895 he introduced a black paper packaging, which facilitated loading and unloading outside a darkened room, and his Pocket Kodak incorporated a small window through which film-positioning numbers could be read. 1898 saw the arrival of the Folding Pocket Kodak, which was to survive for around 60 years. Then, in 1900, came the greatest step of all towards the popularisation of photography – the Box Brownie.

The Brownie was named after pixie-like characters in an internationally popular series of children's stories by the Canadian writer, Palmer Cox. A frog-faced brownie, taking a photograph, illustrated the packaging in which the cameras were sold. No more than a ready-loaded box made of wood and card, the Brownie was held at waist level, was marked on top with a V to assist aiming, and was fitted with a rotary shutter for making the exposure. (A clip-on reflecting viewfinder was soon made available as an optional extra.) The camera cost a mere dollar, or five shillings in Britain. Within a year 100,000 were sold, half of them on the eastern side of the Atlantic. Amateurs everywhere were taking pictures without having to be chemists. There were, of course, those who resented the intrusiveness of the box camera. Indignant gentlemen at the seaside threatened to thrash those cads who sought to take pictures of women in bathing suits. But far more people used the new cameras than objected to them. In 1860, talking of future possibilities, Sir John Herschel had coined the word 'snapshot'. He had died a few years before seeing his vision become a reality, but now the era of the snapshot had arrived.

Glass plate cameras did not disappear. They continued to be used by professionals and serious amateurs well into the new century. But photography was now available to Everyman. Eastman had removed at a stroke the deterrent complications of photography, and this — as much as the low price — was a breakthrough. Many people wanted, and still want, their photography made easy. It is not an unreasonable request, for their interest is in the end product rather than the process. Indeed, the disposable cameras that started to appear towards the end of the 20th century were no more than a revival of Eastman's brilliant marketing idea.

Roll film reigns

Camera ownership had suddenly become affordable for people of very modest means. The little boxes could be taken anywhere, and the introduction of commercially processed roll film had swept away the need for special skills and facilities. Improvements to cameras, film and processing quickly went on to make the revolution secure.

Having made the breakthrough, Eastman's company maintained its impetus. By 1907 it was an international organisation with over 5000 employees. The Box Brownie continued to prosper and on the eve of the Second World War, nearly 40 years after its introduction, it still cost only five shillings. Larger models and a range of folding cameras followed, all with the Brownie name — which continued to be used for the cheapest Kodak cameras until 1980. New technical developments were regularly announced: 1908 saw the opening of an Australian plant for manufacturing the world's first commercially viable safety film (based on cellulose acetate rather than the highly inflammable cellulose nitrate), and the first industrial photographic research laboratory was established in 1913.

But the advances most readily noticed by the general public were those made in cameras, and the Kodak Vest Pocket Camera won a particularly warm welcome. Introduced in 1912, it was a folding camera that, when closed, really was small enough to slip into the pocket. This ready portability helped it become popular very quickly, and the outbreak of the First World War made it seem even more desirable. Many a soldier is said to have taken one of these cameras with him, trusting that it was compact enough to avoid catching the eye of the sergeant major, and the first full year of the war was marked by a huge increase in sales.

When the Kodak Autographic feature was introduced in 1914, it was quickly incorporated into the Vest Pocket model. A small flap was built into the back of the camera, and a removable metal stylus was fitted to the body. The flap opened to reveal a small area of the autographic film's special backing paper, on which the photographer used the stylus to inscribe details of date or subject. Where the backing paper was thus written on, it lost its opacity. Light passed through on to the actual film, and the inscription appeared as black lettering once the film was processed. The writing was done on the narrow strip between images. Thus it appeared on the border of the negatives, but was not transferred to the positives made from them. The feature was exclusive to Kodak and was thought worth including in most of the company's folding cameras until the early 1930s. Its practical effectiveness was limited, both by the reluctance of users to remember to annotate their exposures, and by their ability to mislay the stylus. But the principle of a built-in identification system has been thought good enough in recent years for revival in electronic form, and many cameras can now offer in-frame record of date and time.

As owning cameras became the norm, ways had to be found to refresh their appeal. One such example of re-branding was in the use of colour, and women were the market that was targeted. The aim was to turn the camera into a fashion accessory. In the late 1920s the Number 2 Portrait Brownie was produced in six colour-finishes in addition to the standard black. The Vanity Kodak quickly followed, offering a choice of five colours and a matching silk-lined carrying-case. The Beau Brownie, in 1930, came in only four colour options, but carried an Art Deco design on its front plate. Other manufacturers joined the assault on the fashion-conscious female, and the sales pitch reached its peak with the introduction of matching camera and cosmetic sets. But though women were (and continued to be) an important sector of the market, they showed limited enthusiasm for defining self-image in terms of photographic equipment, and cameras soon reverted to the traditional black.

The entry of Kodak's competitors into the fashion-camera market serves as a reminder that there was more than one company in business, and when new and cheaper materials were introduced, it was one of Eastman's rivals that took the first step. The challenge was to produce cheaper and lighter cameras, and Bakelite offered a solution with the 1928 launch of the Rajar Number 6 Folding Camera, the world's first fully plastic model. For once Kodak was left to follow another's initiative, bringing out its own Bakelite Number 2 Hawkette in 1930. Nevertheless, George Eastman was a pacesetter for many years and, when he died in 1932, he left behind him a company that would continue to innovate.

The box and folding cameras that used roll film thrived, side-by-side, until the Second World War and beyond. The spread of popular models was boosted from the 1920s onward, when makers of cigarettes, chocolate and toiletries offered cameras and films in return for coupons. A free Kodak 120 film, for instance, could be obtained in return for 40 coupons from packets of Black Cat cigarettes, and, in the 1950s, 2700 Kensitas gift certificates would secure a Kodak Junior 1 Folding Camera.

But though the two types of roll film camera dominated the market, they did not share it equally. The folding models with extending bellows were generally favoured by the fairly serious amateurs, who felt at ease with the range of shutter speeds and aperture sizes that such equipment came to provide. The relatively simple box cameras were the more likely choice of those who wanted to make their own pictures, but who made no claim to expertise. These cameras, too, became more sophisticated with the passage of years; but the improvements were of a kind that tended to reassure rather than alarm the technically diffident.

So the box camera survived and flourished up to and through the 1950s, and its typical product was a snapshot, with trademarks that can be found in virtually any family collection. Photos were taken in the open air, because that is where the light was. Users quickly learnt not to point their cameras at the sun, so often made their subjects squint into it instead. Box cameras were held at waist level, and this viewpoint made for a characteristically low horizon. But it had another effect as well. Peering down at tiny reflection in a murky viewfinder did little to bolster the operator's confidence: it was hard to be sure just what was in frame, and it was quite easy to chop off a head or cut out the person at the edge of a group. Such mishaps, along with sloping horizons, occurred frequently enough. But their frequency could be reduced if the camera was kept at a distance from the subjects. So, in the interests of 'getting people all in', photographers often stayed further back than was really necessary, and a small subject against a large background is characteristic of the snapshot. Sometimes this results in a view of house or garden that is of interest to the family historian, but the more frequent outcome is a frustratingly distant view of facial features.

Understandably, not everyone was satisfied by the limited resources of box cameras. Indeed, there were professionals and serious enthusiasts who declined even to convert to roll film. Plate cameras still had their adherents until the 1930s, and when such photographers eventually gave up glass plates it was often in favour of single sheet celluloid film. But their numbers dwindled as roll film offered more and more attractions.

Increasingly sensitive emulsions reduced exposure times, and the 1930s and 1940s saw a steady shift from inflammable nitro-cellulose to safety film. New sizes of film were introduced to fit new models of camera, and the increasingly efficient enlargers of the 1930s brought possibilities of an unprecedented flexibility. Formerly, prints were made by placing the negative over a piece of sensitised paper and exposing the resulting package to light. This meant that a negative had to be big enough to lead to a decent size of print. Films, in their turn, had to provide room for such negatives. But enlargers could project a magnified image of the negative onto the photographic paper. The processor could therefore turn a small negative into a print of much more satisfactory size. This, of course, meant that smaller films could be made. But it also meant that more images could be fitted onto films of existing sizes. As a result, new cameras were designed to give twice as many pictures from a standard film.

An immediate effect was that films became better value for money and had to be changed less frequently. (If the hundred exposures of the earliest roll films had been rather too many, the eight prints offered by some of their successors must have seemed distinctly niggardly, and a doubling of images must have been very welcome.) In the longer term, very small negatives would dominate the popular photographic scene in the later decades of the century.

The professional

Meanwhile, the professional studio had not disappeared. Commercial portrait photographers continued to work with their large format cameras. Glass plates were the norm for the early years of the century, but from 1913 on — when Eastman's Portrait Film came onto the market — the trade gradually made the transition to individual celluloid sheets. The professionals did eventually decline in numbers, but by no means as swiftly as the roll film revolution might lead us to expect.

A survey of photographers and photographic companies listed in Kelly's directories for East Anglia gives an idea of how the professional fared in one part of England. As the 19th century drew to an end, studios were still growing in number. For the counties of Cambridgeshire, Norfolk and Suffolk, 115 operations were listed in 1892, 122 in 1896 and 139 in 1900. What is perhaps surprising is that the arrival of the Box Brownie did nothing to reverse, or even stem, this trend. There were 149 photographers listed in 1904, 161 in 1908, and 167 in 1912. Numbers in Cambridgeshire reached a peak of 34 in 1904, then steadied at 33 for the next two directories. Norfolk and Suffolk reached their maxima of 73 and 61 respectively in 1912. Only in 1916 did a decline start to become evident, with a figure of 146 for the three counties. A steady falling off over the ensuing years led to a total of 123 businesses being recorded in 1925. This position was largely maintained to the end of the decade, with a count of 121 in 1929. Then, in the years leading up to the Second World War, there was a sharp and continuing decline in numbers, with 103 photographers appearing in 1933, and only 82 in 1937. In the period between the wars, the number of professional studios had been halved.

Since ever more people were taking their own photographs, the decline is not hard to account for. Professional portraits were more expensive and less convenient: unlike snatched snaps, they had to be premeditated. So by the 1920s and 1930s a visit to the studio had, as in earlier days, become something of a special occasion to commemorate a milestone in the family's life — a new baby, say, or an engagement or a coming of age. But what is remarkable is that the decline was fended off for so long, and that the commercial practitioner still managed to play a significant role in the years up to the First World War.

The studio remained the best choice for portraits that were recognisable. Snaps had immediacy and could capture the informality of the moment, but they did no great service to the face, for which close-up treatment and adequate lighting were needed. Full-length shots and eyes screwed against the sun (or shadowed by hat brims) characterised snaps, helping to ensure that the professional could still provide something most customers could not make for themselves. The commercial product was better, and that, despite the expense, made it desirable. Ways were devised, too, whereby the cost was made more manageable for the less well-off. Community savings schemes were popular amongst the working classes in the first half of the century. Christmas clubs and loan clubs abounded, organised at the work place or at the pub, and it was natural enough that the principal should be extended to photographs. Members of a cooperative would pay in a penny or two a week and take it in turns to draw on the fund for a visit to the studio. It may now seem a less important event than a birthday or a wedding, but reaching the top of a portrait-club list was, in its own way, a special occasion.

So people still wanted the studio product, and, at least until the First World War, it seems that professional and amateur photographer both found plenty to do. The delay in the studio's decline, despite the runaway success of the box camera, would seem to suggest that, for some years, a greater number of pictures was taken, and that the miles of amateur roll film were exposed in addition to, rather than instead of, the professionals' glass plates.

One important factor in keeping studios busy was a new photographic format — the postcard. The carte de visite and the cabinet print, which had been produced in such vast numbers in the 19th century, were reaching the end of their profitable lives. A few cartes were still being sold, and a few more cabinet prints; but the popular market needed something different. Various new formats were introduced in the early years of the century, but they were merely variations on the theme of an image pasted on a cardboard mount. They may have had a little novelty value, but not enough to capture the mass imagination, and they failed to fit comfortably into the pre-cut apertures of any carte and cabinet print albums that were not yet full. Something wholly different was needed, and the postcard supplied it.

Britain was rather slow to take up the idea of sending pictorial cards through the post. The idea originated from the United States, where plain postcards had been in use since 1867, and where cards decorated with pictures had been introduced in the 1870s. It was not, though, until 1894 that the British authorities recognised the postcard and permitted its use. It quickly became popular. Postcards were convenient, cheap and efficient. The excellent postal service meant that they could even be delivered on the very day that they were posted. So by the end of the century they were in widespread use for arranging visits, advising arrival times, describing holidays and simply maintaining contact. They performed most of the functions that a later generation has thought e-mail was invented for.

The earliest cards had to devote one side (what was then referred to as the front) to the recipient's name and address. Any message and illustration had to share the back. But only a few years into the reign of Edward VII the message space migrated to the other side of the card, where it shared the surface (now thought of as the back) with the address. The whole of the remaining side thus became available for decoration.

Inevitably, people started to send cards for the sake of the pictures they bore, reminding each other of loved places or admired actors, or sharing a taste for sentimental images of children or animals. Equally inevitably, people began to save the cards they had been sent, and publishers of postcards supplied them with a flood of new painted and photographic images. The Victorians had a scrapbook tradition and an inclination for buying cartes or cabinet prints of celebrity sitters and novelty subjects. These tastes were brought very satisfyingly together in the collecting of postcards. As for passing through the post, that became optional. Many cards went into the mail, certainly, but many were acquired simply for the sake of the images they bore.

So in settling on the postcard as the ideal new format, photographers were adopting what was already a winning formula. Other attempts at new formats had lacked a context to fit into. The postcard portrait was instantly part of an environment and was happily in tune with the new age. Of course, professionals still made pictures in other sizes, just as they had always done. But they now, once more, had a product with mass appeal. Copies could be readily given or exchanged, as cartes and cabinet prints had been before them. In fact, these new pictures could even be sent just as they were through the post, should that be required — though the great majority of family photos in this format were never intended for mailing.

The period 1900 to 1918 was the heyday of the postcard as a means of communication. After the First World War delivery charges went up, and postal use decreased. But, as a photographic size, the postcard remained popular throughout the first half of the century. The backs were still divided into message and address spaces, but sitters rarely planned to pop their likenesses in the post box. The postcard, as a format, now enjoyed a vigorous life that was quite independent of the service to which its name referred.

One late stronghold of the professional photographer was the seaside town. As more and more people found themselves able to afford a day trip and, eventually, a full week's holiday, photographers seized the chance to provide a souvenir of the occasion. Tintypes, pictures made of thin sheets of sensitised iron, were offered by some promenade photographers. More popular, though, were postcards. Examples of these (sometimes complete with printed date) often survive in family collections and bear witness to excursions on the sea-front or pier during the years between the two world wars.

Nevertheless, professional practitioners were becoming minor contributors to popular photography. They would survive, continuing to mark special events, and often going out into the world rather than waiting for the world to knock at the studio door. The possibilities of weddings were thoroughly explored; the world of education was tapped, with school and class photos eventually taking second place to the rather more lucrative shots of individual pupils; a useful new market grew up for graduation pictures. But the twentieth century was predominantly the century of the amateur, within whose reach more and more possibilities fell as the years passed.

Many of these possibilities originated in the years before the Second World War, but, in Britain at least, they had to wait for the relative affluence of the 1950s and 1960s before they could really take off.

Moving forward

One development that had to wait a long time for widespread acceptance was 35mm film. Its possibilities were first investigated as early as 1914, but it was not until the mid-twenties that Ernst Leitz designed and marketed his 35mm Leica camera. The response was lukewarm. Many who tried out the small format film found it fiddly to handle and derided it as a toy. A further ten years were to pass before the bakelite Argus Model A camera found some popular acceptance in the States. The introduction in 1936 of 35mm colour transparency film by both Kodak and Agfa helped to consolidate the position of the format, and when the Argus C3 appeared in 1939 it found a ready market and stayed in production for nearly 30 years.

An important refinement of 35mm cameras was the single-lens reflex (SLR) action. This made it possible for the photographer to see exactly the same picture as seen by the lens, instead of having to look through a separate viewfinder. A mirror and prism system enabled the operator to see out through the camera's lens, and the mirror was flicked out of the way at the crucial moment to allow the exposure to be made. The first 35mm SLR camera, the Kine Exactica, was made in Dresden and went on sale in 1937.

Understandably, the market for non-essential consumer goods languished during the Second World War, and luxury items were not high on the agenda during the period of austerity that followed it in Europe. It was, therefore, not until the 1950s that 35mm cameras began to acquire a position of prominence in the UK. The SLR, with its technical sophistication, appealed to the serious amateur and even to the professional, and by the end of the 1960s it had come to dominate this sector of the market. But 35mm cameras were also produced in 'compact' form, with traditional viewfinder and without gadgetry, and this type of model made a strong impact on the upper end of the snapshot market from the 1970s on.

Another development that spanned the war was 'instant' photography. Pioneering work on a while-you-wait, in-camera photographic process was undertaken in Europe at the end of the 1930s. In an adaptation of a process used for document copying, silver halide negative material was used to produce a positive in one stage. But it was Dr Edwin Land of Cambridge, Massachusetts, who eventually marketed a camera that made use of the idea.

Prompted, it is said, by his small daughter's impatience to see pictures that had been taken of her, Land created the Model 95 Polaroid. This squeezed the darkroom chemicals and the separate stages of production within the film layers inside the camera. A large roll of print paper and a smaller roll of negative paper, connected by a leader, were fitted into the top and bottom of the camera back. When the two were brought together and drawn between a pair of rollers, a pod of processing chemicals was broken, and its contents were spread evenly between the two strips. The exposure was made, and a minute was allowed for the chemicals to do their work. The product was removed from the camera through a flap in the back, and, when the protective covering was peeled off, a sepia-coloured print was revealed.

The Polaroid 95 appeared for sale in 1948, and improved versions quickly followed. By 1956, one million Land cameras had been sold worldwide. Nevertheless, these early models were expensive. It took the introduction of colour and the appearance of cheaper cameras, such as the Polaroid Swinger in the 1960s, to make the 'instant' camera an even moderately common weapon in the average family's photographic armoury.

A major refinement of Land's system came in 1972 with the SX-70 camera. This did away with the peel-apart procedure, combining both negative and print components in a sealed unit. As the rollers ejected this unit from the camera, its chemical pod was broken. The processing took place automatically inside a 'dark room' formed by a black pigment layer on the negative's base and a layer of black dye, which subsequently turned transparent to allow the image to be seen through it. Then, in 1976, Kodak entered the field with its own version of instant colour film.

But, despite an eagerness to see results that most photographers share with Land's daughter, it was not 'instant' photography that inherited the mantle of the box camera. That role was to be filled by the Instamatic.

Introduced by Kodak in 1963, the Instamatic used a new small-format film, the 126, which came ready packed in a plastic cartridge. This did away with the need to find subdued lighting for loading the camera, and there was no struggling to feed the film's leader into a slot in a spool. The user simply opened the back of the camera, dropped the cartridge into the vacant space, and closed the camera again. When the film was fully exposed, the cartridge was slipped out and passed over for processing. No skill was needed. (There were still unconfident photographers who took their cameras into the shop for loading or unloading, but their self-doubt really was misplaced.)

The Instamatic was an enormous success, and it was accompanied by 126 colour films for both slides and prints. This had implications for processing and marked the beginning of the end for the black-and-white developing and printing service run by local chemists. The rather more complicated colour processing was now undertaken by large, dedicated laboratories, which used the chemists simply as delivery and collection points, or which conducted their business by post.

Attempts to follow the Instamatic and to build on its strengths were less convincing. In 1972 Kodak launched the Pocket Instamatic, which used 110 film cartridges. Improvements in film quality had reached the point where reasonably satisfactory enlargements could be made from very small negatives, and 110 film, with its 19 x 13 mm negatives, sought to take advantage of this. But some users found the enlargements grainy and indistinct, and this strengthened the case of those companies — with Japanese manufacturers prominent among them — who were promoting the larger format 35mm compact cameras. Nevertheless, there was one further attempt to convince the public that, in the case of negatives, small is beautiful. In 1982 Kodak unveiled its Disc Camera, which abandoned roll film in favour of a revolving disc from which 15 tiny (10 x 8 mm) negatives were produced. Take-up was disappointing, and production of these cameras ceased after only six years.

Other developments in the later years of the century included an increasing amount of automation on 35mm cameras, both SLR and compact, as well the appearance of panoramic cameras, APS (advanced photo system) cameras and digital imaging. But the mere mention of these is the most that can be justified in a work that focuses on old photographs.

Light and colour

Of the aids and devices that have been added to cameras, artificial lighting is important for the difference it has made to the kind of picture that the amateur photographer can take. If a usable image is to result, sensitised film must be exposed to just the right amount of light. Too much illumination can be avoided by making the light pass through a small enough aperture and by closing that aperture quickly, and simple cameras could manage that quite easily. Problems arose, however, if the light was too weak. The longer the aperture was left open, the longer both subject and photographer had to keep still. The professional could furnish a studio with a battery of strong lights designed for the purpose, but ordinary domestic lighting was too weak to take snaps by. So interior shots were out of the question for the non-specialist until the arrival of the flash bulb.

The first flash bulbs — which replaced the earlier and rather dangerous flash powder — were unveiled in Germany in 1925 by Paul Vierkölter. They lacked refinement, for the procedure involved a series of separate operations: opening the shutter, firing the flash, and then closing the shutter. They were also expensive. So at first they were no more the salvation of the unpretending amateur than flash powder had been. But systems were improved, bulbs became smaller and cheaper, and by the mid-1930s professional and advanced amateur cameras boasted synchronised shutters and automatic firing. The first popular camera to feature flash was the Falcon Press Flash in 1939, and it was followed a year later by Kodak's first entry into this field with the Six-20 Flash Brownie.

Nevertheless, as with other advances, widespread use had to wait until after the war. It was not until the 1950s that popular cameras were routinely designed to take flash, and even then the option was not necessarily used, for it meant investing in a flashgun to attach to the camera and buying a supply of bulbs, each of which could be used only once. A repeatable electronic flash had been invented by Harold Egerton in the 1930s, but it was not until the 1960s that electronic units began to make an impression on the market. In fact, the more popular option during the Instamatic era was the flashcube, which gave a burst of light from four successive faces before it had to be discarded.

Increasing the dose of light that reaches the film is one way of taking photographs indoors. The other possibility is to use more sensitive (or 'faster') film: the more quickly the treated surface reacts to the light, the shorter exposure it needs. Kodak introduced its high-speed Tri-X black and white film in 1954, but a wait of over 20 years was necessary before flash-free indoor colour photographs were a realistic proposition for the layman. In 1976 Fuji introduced an ASA400 colour print film (the higher the ASA number, the faster the film), and Agfa and Kodak quickly followed suit. But though natural-light indoor photography had become a possibility, the overwhelming popular preference remained with flash.

The other major addition to the photographer's resources during the century was the use of colour. It had been long aspired to. The tinting of prints by hand had been practised ever since the 1840s, and attempts to build colour into the processing stage date from James Clerk Maxwell's 1861 demonstration of the colour separation process. He showed that the primary colours of light (red, blue and green) could be separately recorded and then brought together to produce a polychromatic image. But his method was dreadfully cumbersome, as was the beam-splitting camera devised by Frederick Ives in the 1890s.

The first practical colour method that was suitable for anything approaching widespread use was the Autochrome process. This was announced by the Lumière brothers in 1904 and marketed in 1907. It involved dusting a glass plate with a mixture of red-, blue- and green-dyed grains of potato starch before applying a standard photographic emulsion. The grains acted as tiny colour filters, enacting the three-part colour separation process at one time on one plate. The result was a coloured glass transparency with rather soft and muted tones. It was then either projected or looked at in a hand-held viewer.

Naturally, other experiments followed. But the Lumières' process continued to be used into the 1930s. Only then did convenient and reliable colour film arrive to replace it. Indeed, several companies launched products very close together in the middle of the decade. Dufaycolor film was introduced first in France and then in the UK, and Gasparcolor came from Germany. But it was Kodachrome and Agfacolor that made what were to prove to be the most lasting impressions. Whilst each of these had its own system, both used the concept of a tri-pack film, where three different chemical layers, each sensitive to only one colour of light, were incorporated onto a single sheet of film. Kodak was quick to explore the possible applications and, from 1935 to 1936, introduced its film in various sizes and in both still and motion picture formats.

But, as with other advances, the intervention of war impeded the spread of colour photography, and the production of home movie film for civilian use was halted. New still colour films appeared during the war, among them Ansco, Sakura, and an improved version from Agfa. In the States, Kodak brought out Kodacolor, a colour negative film that gave prints rather than slides, and this was to become enormously popular. But its impact in the UK was considerably delayed.

New brand names and new lines continued to appear in the immediate post-war years. Kodak's Ektachrome, introduced in 1946 and manufactured in Britain from the early 1950s, was the company's first colour film that could be processed by the photographer. It became the common choice of those professionals who were making the transition to colour. Ferraniacolor also won some adherents among amateur processors at the end of the 1940s. The actual representation of colour during these years (and even, to a degree, into the 1960s) tended to be more bold than subtle, with golden yellows and nail-varnish reds. Portraits often had a slightly raw and unnatural look.

Public enthusiasm in the UK was measured. Colour negative film took a modest share of the market from the early 1950s, and transparencies attracted their devotees as people began to travel abroad. The availability of Kodacolor in 35mm format from 1958 helped colour to consolidate its position, but at the end of the 1950s colour — whether for slides or prints — was still largely the province of the enthusiast. It was only in the 1960s that it really took off. After all, the 1960s were (though not immediately) the decade of colour: at its beginning the quality Sunday papers started to publish colour supplements, and by its end the BBC had begun colour television transmissions. Clothes, cars and design shrugged off their monochrome sobriety, and photography followed suit. For the amateur photographer, the arrival of the Instamatic was the significant factor: drop-in cartridges and mass-processing labs made it easy to take snapshots that were in tune with the colourfulness of the times.

Black-and-white photography took a while to die, and many photographers kept it in their repertoire alongside colour for some time. But by the end of 1970, colour films were outselling their black-and-white counterparts in the UK in a ratio of ten to one. Increasing uniformity of chemical processes meant that different films produced, to most eyes, similarly authentic results. Colour was a little slow to catch on, but the change, when it came, was decisive.

Dating the Artefact — Prints

Processes

If a photographic process can be recognised, the period over which it was used can give the first clue to the date of the picture it has produced. There are two drawbacks to this proposition. Processes are not always as easy to identify as one would wish, and some were in use over many years. But any piece of evidence for dating, however wide in years its implications are, may play its part in nudging us towards a conclusion. It is, therefore, worth looking at some of the more easily distinguished processes.

Carbon prints

Carbon printing was introduced in the 1860s, but it continued in use well into the 20th century. It gave strong colours, and was capable of good gradation of tones as well as sharp contrasts. Although images could be produced in red, blue, green or black, dark brown was the most usual. Attempts to describe tones of brown (rich, warm, sepia, umber, and so on) can easily founder on the rocks of differing perceptions, but it is fair to say that a dense intensity is characteristic of the darkest tones of a carbon print. There is a smooth sheen to the finish, but it stops well short of high gloss. Also helpful is the fact that, when the surface is viewed at an angle, there can sometimes be a slight relief effect where dark and light areas meet, as if the image has been painted on. The effect is easy to exaggerate, so its apparent absence should not be relied on as disproof. But discerning its presence can provide a welcome confirmation of one's thoughts. Carbon prints, including some patented variations of the process, were still being produced as late as the 1930s. (The Autotype Company, for instance, continued marketing its carbon tissue until late in the decade.)

Platinum prints

Though it could be produced as a sepia image, the platinum print (or platinotype) is most often recognised by its full and subtle range of greys. These often have a silvery quality in their lighter tones, and the overall effect is of some softness and delicacy. The matt, non-reflective surface is also a useful identification feature. The paper was impregnated (rather than coated) with the light sensitive chemicals, and this helped make it particularly resistant to fading. Sometimes, however, residual specks of metal may have caused rust-coloured stains to appear on the surface. First produced in the 1870s, platinotypes survived into the 1930s. But such late examples are rare. The platinum for which they were named was the key ingredient in their production, and its cost rose sharply at the end of the First World War. The process was therefore too expensive to form a routine part of the ordinary photographer's repertoire after about 1917 or 1918.

Tintypes
The tintype, or ferrotype, was another process that carried over from the previous century, having been introduced in the 1850s. The image was formed on a very thin, blackened sheet of iron that had been coated with photographic emulsion. If unframed, a tintype is, therefore, instantly recognisable. Even if it has been put in a frame or case, it is usually fairly easy to discern that it is made of metal. It is much lighter than the daguerreotype or the ambrotype — the Victorian cased images with which it could conceivably be confused. If there is any doubt, a fridge magnet applied to its back will soon show whether the image is on an iron base. Never as popular in the UK as it was in the United States, the tintype survived into the 20th century as a cheap process used by seaside and travelling photographers. Examples from the years before the First World War are not rare, and the occasional promenade or country fair tintype may be found to date from the years between the wars.

Opal prints
One further possible survival from Victorian times is the opal print, or opaltype. These attractive pictures on white translucent glass were first produced in the 1860s. Unframed examples present no difficulties of identification, and even if they are framed, the nature of the base material is still likely to be evident. Opal prints were never produced in vast quantities, but some were still being made until about 1920.

Developing out papers

In use for printing from the 1880s, 'developing out' paper became the standard photographic paper for professional use from around 1900. Artificial light was directed through the negative and onto the paper for a few seconds, during which time a latent image formed on it. This image was then brought out in a chemical bath, before being immersed in a fixing agent.

There were several different types of developing out paper, and sheets varied in thickness and surface finish, so identification is not always possible. But there are a few clues to be looked for.

Silver bromide (or gelatin bromide, or bromide) developing out paper can often be identified by a silvery, grape-like bloom in the darker areas of the image. This has built up over the years, as moisture has been absorbed by gelatin in the emulsion and affected its silver content. (If pollution in the atmosphere has tarnished the silver, the effect will be more bronzed than glaucous.) Paper coated with a gelatin and silver emulsion continued in use until displaced by modern polyethylene papers. Nevertheless, it is often possible to identify the earlier silver bromide prints: they had a soft, slaty quality to the black tones, and this is often evident in pictures from before the First World War.

Chloro-bromide developing out paper is often described as having a softness of effect, with dark grey rather than dense black as the deepest tone. This may not be entirely helpful, however, since it may be hard to know whether one is recognising a diagnostic quality or just seeing the results of slight underdevelopment or fading. Though available since the beginning of the century, this paper didn't become really popular until about 1920. It then enjoyed its market share for some 30 years.

Rather more useful information can perhaps be given about chloride (or silver chloride, or gelatino-chloride) developing out paper. This, the most frequently encountered type, could give good black tones — though fading or yellowing may by now have weakened them. The paper reacted slowly enough to be handled in subdued light, and this accounts both for its popularity and for its being often referred to as 'gaslight' paper. It was widespread from Edwardian times and in common use until the 1950s. What makes it easily recognisable, however, is the fact that its trade name is often to be found printed on the back: 'Velox' for the Kodak product and 'Selo' for Ilford.

The study of these names on photographs of known date suggests that the design may carry its own dating message, though conclusions must remain rather tentative until they have been tested against many more examples.

Sometimes 'VELOX' appears printed entirely in upper case; but more often only the 'V' appears as a capital and the whole word is enclosed in an oval outline. A wholly upper case example has been found from as late as 1946, but the vast majority of examples come from the late 1920s and the first half of the 1930s. The more common enclosed logo comes in three easily identifiable forms. The most usual measures about 12 x 6 mm, and the 'V' is fairly plain (rather like the italic form of the Perpetua font). Examples examined so far span a period from mid-1920s to mid-1950s. But a variant version of the same size is characterised by more florid lettering and a distinct flourish to the right-hand stroke of the 'V'. This design seems to have emerged at the very end of the 1920s and to have fallen from favour by the middle of the 1930s. The third enclosed version has a similar flourish but is larger, measuring about 18 x 7 mm. It seems (on very limited evidence) to be associated with the late 1920s. Finally, a very late design is made up of three unenclosed words — 'Kodak Velox Paper' — printed one under the other. Examples have been found from the second half of the 1950s and even as late as 1962.

The Ilford logos present a rather simpler picture. From the later 1920s until the early 1940s 'SELO' routinely appeared in serif-free upper case inside a diamond-shaped outline measuring 18 x 12 mm. But a smaller version of the same design, 10 x 7 mm, has also been encountered and seems to belong only to the 1940s.

It must, however, be emphasised that these observations on logos represent theory-in-progress. Further investigation may serve to strengthen, modify or completely undermine the conclusions so far drawn.

Printing out papers

'Printing out' paper (commonly referred to as P.O.P.) used natural light. Placed under the negative, it was exposed to daylight for several minutes. During this time the areas beneath the clear parts of the negative darkened and an image was formed. No separate developing procedure was needed, and the print simply needed to be fixed in the normal way to stop the darkening process from going any further. It had been in use for part of the 19th century, but it came into its own in the age of the amateur processor, for whom it simplified operations significantly. The method was used for contact prints, and where glass negatives were used, a visible rim at the very edges of the picture may show how light has passed through the thickness of the glass.

Prints are generally fairly glossy, with colour (special effects apart) in the reddish-brown to dark brown range. They have proved very susceptible to fading, but though the darker areas turn to yellow, the highlights tend to remain white.

There were two sorts of printing out paper, and it will often prove impossible to distinguish between them. Gelatino-chloride P.O.P. — trade-named Solio Paper in its Kodak version — may be a little more likely to have developed tiny cracks in the emulsion. It could be hand-coloured, and it remained popular with amateur processors until the 30s. Prints on collodio-chloride P.O.P. have sometimes acquired yellow spots as they have aged. They were not amenable to colouring. Though collodio-chloride P.O.P. lasted a little longer — until the end of the 1930s — its main use in its later years was for professionals' proofs.

Modern papers
The old developing out paper was replaced by resin-coated, or polyethylene, paper from about 1970. The resin stops the paper becoming soaked through, so surplus chemicals can be rinsed quickly off the surface, and the sequence of processes (developing, fixing, washing) takes much less time. Such paper, easily recognised by the rather plastic feel of the back, must be modern — though it may, of course, bear old images of which copies have been made.

Polaroid prints
The first Land camera, the Model 95, went on sale in 1948. It used a Type 40 picture roll, which gave 8 deckle-edged, sepia-coloured prints. The overall print size was 3¼ x 4¼ inches (8.3 x 10.8 cm), but the actual image area measured only 2⅞ x 3¾ inches (7.3 x 9.5 cm). This gave rather wide borders,

especially at the bottom of the picture, where the depth could be up to ⅝ inch (1.7cm).

Type 40 film was produced for only a couple of years before being replaced in 1950 by Type 41, which gave a black and white image. Fading proved to be a particular problem at first, but this was quickly addressed by providing a 'print coater' to fix the image. Particularly faded examples of pictures from this film are therefore likely to belong to its earliest years.

Colour was introduced in 1963 with Type 48 film, though some users felt its balance and quality did not match up to the 35mm colour film of the time. Early pictures from Type 48 films were very subject to curling, because the tensions within the print's chemical layers changed over a period of time. Films were sold with a set of self-adhesive mounting cards to counter the problem. Lack of curl or mounting card doesn't automatically prove a photo dates from the later years of Type 48, but it does offer a possibility worth considering. Mounting cards were still being provided in 1966, and may have continued until about 1970.

There was also a 30 series of Polaroid films, which produced 2½ x 3¼ inch (6.3 x 8.3 cm) prints, with an image area of 2⅛ x 2⅞ inches (5.4 x 7.3 mm). This series was introduced in 1954, and a colour version followed in 1963.

1963 also saw the arrival of pack (rather than roll) films, and these gave the same sizes as Type 40 films. Later pack and roll films might reasonably be considered too modern for detailed treatment, but it is worth noting that Polaroid pictures with a black patch on the back are an indication of the SX-70 system. This replaced peel-apart technology and made its début in 1972.

Early formats
Just as some processes carried over from one century to the next, so did some formats. Cartes de visite and cabinet prints were about to lose their domination of the market, but they still had a few years of life in them.

Cartes de visite were prints measuring about 3½ x 2¼ inches (9 x 5.8 cm), pasted to a card mount of around 4 x 2½ inches (10.2 x 6.4 cm). They were in decline by the beginning of the century and being produced in much smaller numbers than cabinet prints. But Edwardian examples can still be found. Family albums had, for years, been furnished with pre-cut apertures of a size to take cartes and cabinet prints, and all the time there were still gaps in their albums, customers retained some interest in the older formats. This residual demand accounts for the fact that, in the years just before the First World War, some photographers were producing carte-sized unmounted prints. They were not the same as cartes, for they had no stout backing and their image, apart from a modest white border, took up the whole space. But they fitted very conveniently into a family's existing storage and display system.

Cabinet prints, too, had only a short time left to them. By the beginning of the century they had become more popular than cartes, but the advent of postcard format and mass camera ownership combined to undermine their position. Like cartes, they were prints mounted on card, but their dimensions were larger. Sizes varied slightly, but the image measured approximately 4 x 5½ inches (10 x 14 cm), and the mount was in the region of 4½ x 6½ inches (11.5 x 16.5 cm). Edwardian cabinet prints are not numerous, but nor are they rare. Examples from the early Georgian years, just before the First World War, are not unknown.

Both cartes and cabinet prints are easy to identify. Where there is a problem, it may lie in deciding whether they date from the 19th or 20th century. Fortunately, fashions in mount design are of some help.

During the 1880s and 1890s mounts became increasingly sumptuous. Elaborate, often pictorial designs, covered their backs. Then came a taste for dark and dramatic card colours. Bottle green, maroon and black were particularly popular, and, to show up against these colours, the printing had to be in white, silver or gold. Edges were bevelled and often touched with silver or gold. The effect was one of richness. Admittedly, some mount designers started to leave the back blank, perhaps finding the expanse of dark card too overwhelming for their graphic fancies. But opulence remained the message conveyed by these mounts.

As the 1890s progressed, however, a reaction set in: a new sobriety of mount design emerged, and the flowers, birds and cherubs gave way to a little elegant lettering. Pale card was used again — white, off-white and cream. The printing, though contrasting with the base colour, might be a little muted. Black was quite possible, but greys and dark browns also found favour. Gold and silver might also still be used, but there was something restrained about using them on, say, a cream rather than a maroon background. The overall effect was still of richness, but the riches were not ostentatiously displayed. The second half of the 1890s seems to have been the main period of change, though some photographers opted very quickly for the new style of mounts, and others were in no hurry to become converted to the nouveau chaste school of thought.

As the feeling for cool dignity took firmer hold, further refinements became popular. The card surface was now often matt rather than glossy, and it was often given — in part at least — a textured finish. Borders might be impressed around the print area, and the space between them might be cross-hatched or given the look of pebbledash or vermicelli. Slightly darker colours might be used, but they were still subdued, and the palette extended from the white and cream range to include shades of grey, fawn and even soft and dusty green. Brown, though darker than the other favoured colours, was also unassertive enough to be an occasional choice. Lettering tended towards low contrast, with gold, silver, grey and brown (even quite pale brown) all proving popular. Sometimes the lettering was pressed into the card rather than simply printed on the surface. In such cases, colour might be used to highlight the effect, but the mere impression in the card was often thought enough. However the wording was presented, there was not much of it. The photographer and studio address might be identified along the bottom border, and sometimes a monogram, formed from the practitioner's initials, might be added. This could be imprinted, embossed, or even given a touch of colour. The back, however, was generally left quite unadorned. Bevelled edges were still quite possible, but deckle or scalloped edges also came into vogue. Many of these tastes in mount design can be seen on the latest examples of cartes and, in particular, cabinet prints (which offered a little more room for texturing). They also characterised mounts of other picture-sizes in the Edwardian period.

The dating implications of these shifts in fashion can be summed up in general terms: mounts on dark card usually date from the 19th century; smooth and glossy mounts in the understated idiom could belong to either century, though the earlier one is rather more likely; matt or textured understated mounts almost always date from the 20th century.

As cartes and cabinet prints came to seem rather old-fashioned, there were attempts to introduce photographs in new sizes. Novelty formats had occasionally been launched in the 19th century without any great or lasting success, and the 20th century saw a few more such attempts. Their most common characteristic was a more than usually elongated rectangular shape. Panel prints enjoyed a brief period of favour in the 1900s, cornering a share of the market for pictures of actresses and other celebrities that postcards had begun to cater to. They measured 5¾ x 1¾ inches (14.6 x 4.5 cm). (There is some room for confusion, though, as 'panel print' was also used as a name for rather larger mounted pictures of 8¼ x 4 inches, or 21 x 10.2 cm). Another Edwardian format, the coupon print, came as a strip of upright rectangles, each about 3½ x 1½ inches (8.9 x 3.8 cm). Another experiment from these years produced unmounted prints that were 1¼ inches wide and 1½ inches high (3.2 x 3.8 cm), though a narrow border at the top, bearing the studio address, meant that the actual image was close to square. These little prints were fitted into specially designed albums, which could be slipped into pocket or handbag.

Not very many of such novelty items survive in family collections, because none of them caught on as firmly as their creators must have hoped for. It was the postcard that was to prove the truly popular successor to the carte de visite and cabinet print.

Roll film pictures

Very early forms of roll film were made of oiled, sensitised paper or from gelatin emulsion with a paper backing from which it was later stripped off for processing. But it was with the celluloid roll film that snapshot photography really took off, and with the Box Brownie that it became a commonplace activity. Thus, whilst roll film pictures could date from the last years of the nineteenth century, in practice we may reasonably think of them as a 20th century phenomenon. Then they became widespread. Indeed, unless they are obviously professional products, or unless there was a very serious ancestor still using glass plates and doing his or her own processing, it is reasonable to suppose that 20th century pictures in the family collection were taken on roll film.

If there is any doubt that a photograph originates from roll film, the following points might be borne in mind. Roll film pictures were generally taken out of doors, because they depended on the availability of bright, natural light. Whilst professionals could make enlargements from the beginning of the century, such treatment of amateurs' snaps was not was not particularly common until well after the First World War. So fairly early roll film prints tend to be relatively small — often less than postcard size. They are also unlikely to be individually mounted, (though they may have been stored in albums designed to accommodate prints from that particular film size). Finally, roll film prints are liable to show the timeless limitations of snapshot photographs. Indeed, they may show some of them to a greater degree than we would experience today. Whilst we, as photographers, are still quite capable of standing too far away, scalping our subjects or tilting horizons, many modern cameras give us a lot of help. They make decisions about the regulation of light that were formerly made by the operator, or that were simply not there for the making. So washed-out or (more frequently) over-dark images are further common features of early roll film pictures.

In theory, size can help in dating pictures printed from roll film negatives. In practice, the position is complicated by a number of factors: new negative sizes were constantly being introduced; old sizes were given a further lease of life by being used in new equipment; cameras were devised which recorded two photographs on the same length of film that was previously used for one. There is the further possibility that the image size of the surviving picture may not be that of the original negative. From the 1920s onward there is an increasing chance that it may have been enlarged. Since the edges of the image may have been lost in the enlarging, the measurements of the resulting print may not even be in proportion to those of the original negative.

Thus, though precise information can be given about the introduction of new film sizes, print size may prove less helpful for dating than might be hoped. It is, though, worth considering. Many snapshots are contact prints, and contact prints relate directly in size to the film from which they derive. A few brief points and some generalisations can therefore be offered here. The reader is also referred to the consideration of negatives in the next chapter, and to the negative-size dating chart near the end of the book.

The first Brownies, launched in 1900, gave 2¼ inch (5.7 cm) square images. In 1901 (some sources give 1902, but Kodak says 1901 and should know), the Number 2 Brownie introduced the 2¼ x 3¼ inch (5.7 x 8.3 cm) snapshot. This size was to prove enormously popular, and it survived for over half a century. Another popular size, introduced in 1912, was 2½ x 1⅝ inches (6.4 x 4.2 cm), as given by 127 film in the Kodak Vest Pocket camera. This camera remained in production until the mid 1920s. But the film survived much longer, particularly for use in the Brownie 127, a bakelite camera that became a very common choice for first-time buyers.

So far the concern has been with box cameras, but roll film folding cameras had also appeared in the late 1890s, and they enjoyed a limited degree of favour in the years before the First World War. Generally, folding cameras could give larger negatives than their box relations, and one early model took full-plate pictures, 8½ x 6½ inches (21.6 x 16.5 cm). Such a size required too cumbersome a camera for easy use, and quarter plate (3¼ x 4¼ inches or 8.3 x 10.8 cm) and postcard (3¼ x 5½ inches or 8.3 x 14 cm) were more common picture sizes for roll film folding cameras in the first fifteen years of the twentieth century. It was, though, not until the 1930s that the folding camera really came into its own, so examples of its roll film photographs tend more often to date from this later period.

If the 1930s saw a boom in larger roll film pictures, they also saw an increase in small negatives. The Box Tengor gave sixteen pictures, 2¼ x 1¼ inches (5.7 x 3.3 cm), from films that had previously produced eight snaps. The Baby Tengor used 127 film, but gave pictures, which measured 1¼ x 1½ inches (3.3 x 3.8 cm). Small negatives were, of course, a more reasonable proposition once enlargement was widely practised.

So, in very general terms, the position with contact prints may be summed up thus: very few roll film pictures are earlier than 1900, and most are Edwardian or later. Contact prints measuring 2½ x 1⅝ inches (6.4 x 4.2 cm) are not earlier than 1912. The larger sizes tend, in general, to date from after (often well after) the Great War, but postcard and quarter plate pictures could come from the years immediately before it.

Later roll films, such as those for 35mm cameras, Instamatics and pocket Instamatics, gave small pictures that relied on enlargement. But, while contact prints are being considered — and for the sake of completeness — mention might be made of a practice adopted by some postal labs when processing Instamatic film. They hit on the idea of returning, on one piece of photographic paper, an enlargement of a picture flanked by two or three contact-sized versions of it. These small images, measuring about 1⅛ inches

(2.9 cm) square, could be snipped off and given to family and friends. The idea became popular a little while after the launch of Instamatics, so examples are likely to date from the late 1960s or the 1970s. They may be recognised both by their size and (anticipating the next section of this chapter) by the fact that they are in colour.

Colour prints

Whilst early colour prints may be recognised by their uncertain colour values (rather muted at first, but over-bright in the 1950s), it is not suggested different films can be identified by the ways in which they mimicked the sky or reproduced flesh tones. But since processes and manufacturers may sometimes be identified by a trade name on the back of a print or even the original packing in which they were returned to the photographer, it is worth noting when certain names entered the field.

Dufaycolor roll film was introduced in France in 1935 and the UK in 1936, when a sheet film version also became available. Ferraniacolor appeared in the late 1940s and won some adherents amongst amateur processors. Whilst Kodak was marketing colour slide film from 1936, it was not until around 1950 that Kodacolor print film became available in the UK. Agfacolor print film was launched at around the same time. In 1958, Kodacolor made its first appearance in 35mm format.

Nevertheless, as the 1960s dawned, colour was still predominantly something for the enthusiast with a greater interest in slides than prints. It was the advent of the Instamatic that changed everything, and most colour prints in most family albums date from 1963 or later.

Lighting

It is usually possible to decide whether flash has been used in an indoor picture. One sign is flat and rather harsh front lighting, so that the highlights close to the camera appear unnaturally white. Bright foregrounds may contrast sharply with dark backgrounds, rather than fade gently away into an unremarkable gloom. Reflections may be given off by smooth and shiny surfaces — jewellery, polished furniture, windows, glazed pictures and spectacles. Sharp shadows often appear under noses and chins (and, in colour pictures, there may be the red-eye effect, where light has hit the subject's retina and bounced back as a baleful scarlet dot).

Such effects are possible but rare in pictures from the thirties. Though the earliest flashbulbs appeared in Germany in 1929 and electronic flash was developed in the USA in 1939, flash was a post-war facility for most amateur photographers. Some used it in the 1940s, but it was not at all common until well into the 1950s. From the 1960s onwards flash became much more popular, and colour flash pictures came into most people's lives as a result of the Instamatic boom.

Some indoor pictures, although clearly taken in the home rather than the studio, are well lit. They have adequate illumination without the flatness of unrelieved front lighting. These images serve as a reminder that some dedicated amateurs contrived their own lighting systems, with bulbs set in polished biscuit tins that served as reflectors. But occasional indoor pictures may seem to have been taken without the help of artificial light. These may show the subject posed to make the most of the light coming through a window. They may be rather dimly illuminated, and the shadows may seem deep on the unlit side of the subject and in parts of the room not directly hit by the sun's rays. But there will still be a softness of effect and a modelling of form and features that flash pictures are likely to lack. The discovery of such flash-free indoor pictures in the family collection is, incidentally, an indication of a fairly serious photographer, for they needed a camera capable of giving good control over aperture size and length of exposure.

Black and white films capable of recording scenes in the sunnier parts of a room were introduced by Kodak in 1954 and Land's Polaroid company in 1956. The Type 47 Polaroid film, which appeared in 1959, had a speed of ASA 3000 (and this was at a time when even ASA 200 was thought fast). The first ASA 400 colour print film had to wait until 1976, when it was introduced by Fuji. Agfa and Kodak quickly followed suit.

The Professional Product

Though the postcard quickly occupied a particular niche in the professional's repertoire, there was some call in Edwardian times for the larger mounted print. Quarter plate, or 4 x 5 inches (10.2 x 12.7 cm) was a standard size for the first half of the century, but something bigger was always possible, and was particularly suited to the group portraits that became popular from Edwardian times on.

Through the reign of Edward VII, and on to the outbreak of the First World War, the prevailing taste in mounts was that which had developed for cartes and cabinet prints. Matt card of a pale or subdued colour was the usual choice. White was possible (indeed, white was never impossible), and so were off-white, cream, fawn, buff and pale grey. Darker greys, sober browns and dusty greens were also sometimes used. A series of borders, each a little larger than its predecessor, might be pressed into the card to surround the print, and texturing might give variety to the surface. Ample scope for such effects was offered by mounts which were much larger than the prints they displayed, and which presented wider borders than had been usual with cartes and cabinet prints. Trade information on mounts was now minimal. The photographer or studio might be identified, often quite unobtrusively at the bottom, but even that much text was not to be taken for granted. Mounts were generally produced with blank backs, though a label or some form of annotation might occasionally be added.

After the First World War the mount was rarely informative or rich in design interest. Photographic papers had become more robust, and pictures could simply be slipped into a protective folder. There was now no need to stick them to stout card, though the white or cream frame-style mount never completely disappeared. More characteristic of the 1920s and 1930s, though, was the fold-over card. A little larger than the print it held, this had small pre-cut slots in its back half. The corners of the print were slid into these slots, and the front of the folder was closed to protect the image. Sometimes, but by no means always, these folders bore the name and address of the photographer. A decorative motif on the front might, as a dating aid, suggest the art deco style, but many folders were quite plain. This way of presenting photographs continued to prove of some use for the rest of the century.

Though professionals were capable of using it earlier, colour gained widespread use among them no more quickly than among the rest of the population. It may be that, in a world that was becoming determinedly polychromatic, a certain sense of refinement and artistry adhered to pictures made in black and white. At any rate, professional colour portraits are generally likely to date from the later 1960s or after.

Another dimension of professional work was the processing of amateurs' pictures. The processing chains, with a central laboratory fed by a network of collection and distribution agents, grew up in the 1960s. Before that, studios and chemists' shops undertook their own processing. In the 1950s and earlier, therefore, prints were routinely returned to the customer in the local processor's envelope. Where such envelopes have survived (as personal experience suggests they sometimes do), the checking of name and address against trade directories may help in narrowing down the date. One would, however, want to see some corroborating evidence from the prints or negatives themselves, since the photos now stored in an old shop envelope are not necessarily the ones that were originally presented in it, fifty or more years ago.

Comparing photographers' names and addresses with trade directory entries can be a great aid towards dating. Some businesses continued in the same hands and at the same address for many years, but others came and went, moved premises, took on new partners, or passed from parent to child. Sometimes a particular combination of name and studio address (or addresses) held good for only a few years, and the changes that occurred may be reflected in trade directory entries. Unfortunately 20th century mounts tended to be less informative than those of earlier years, but any trade information on mount or packaging is worth checking out.

There are, however, fewer short cuts than there are for Victorian studios. Lists of early photographic studios exist for some areas, and these can save much laborious leafing through a series of trade directories. Some of these lists have been privately published; a few have been sponsored by libraries, museum services or similar bodies; and the Historical Group of the Royal Photographic Society has been particularly active in the field. But such aids tend to stop at a point that is not far into the new century. Some, in fact, only cover the period to 1900. Rather more of them deal with Edwardian as well as Victorian photographers. A number cover the First World War, and a very few stretch to the beginning of the Second. Such coverage of the 20th century is valuable, but it is sadly limited.

Postcards

Although picture postcards did not become an authorised form of postal traffic until late in 1894, they very quickly became popular as a method of communication. Between April 1st 1903 and March 31st 1904, 700 million of them were delivered in Great Britain. But, away from the post-box, the postcard speedily took on an independent life of its own as a photographic format. If it was suitable for mass-produced portraits of the famous, it was just as suitable for one or two copies of the picture of an ordinary sitter. If the photographic stock happened to be printed up with a divided back and a little rectangle showing where a stamp should go, that did not mean that the end product had to be posted. It could be, and it often was. People quickly picked up the idea of sending postcard pictures of themselves to distant friends and relatives. But postcard portraits were just as likely to go straight into an album, without any thought of their being mailed.

Because private portraits were commonly produced in the form of sendable cards, they can often be the more easily dated. One caveat should be sounded, however. Just as the presence of a well-known figure in a carte de visite album does not mean that the VIP was part of the family, so the appearance of an ancestor in a format used for souvenirs of stage and music hall stars does not mean that the family produced a celebrity.

Size can be of some help in dating the earlier examples of postcard. Though it is not foolproof, it can at least serve to distinguish the century of origin. The still common 5½ x 3½ inches (14 x 9 cm) card dates from November 1899. Smaller cards, such as 5¼ x 3¼ inches (13.3 x 8.3 cm) or the 4½ x 3½ inches (11.5 x 9 cm) 'court' card, are likely to date from the second half of the 1890s. The change to the new size in 1899 was not immediate, of course, and postcards have frequently been produced in non-standard sizes since then. For early postcards, however, a pre- or post-1899 dating may be based on measurements with a fair degree of probability.

Whilst 5½ x 3½ inches was to remain the standard size, all manner of dimensions were tried out over the ensuing years until, in 1926, maximum and minimum sizes were adopted for postal acceptability. Cards were to measure between 4 and 2¾ inches (10.2 and 7 cm) along the shorter side, and between 5⅞ and 4⅛ inches (14.9 and 10.5 cm) on the longer side. These regulations allowed quite a lot of room for variation. But if a postcard outside these limits is encountered, it is fair to conclude that (if not obviously modern) it dates from 1926 or earlier.

The backs of postcards can also prove informative. The divided back was not authorised until 1902 in Britain. Before that date the whole of one side had to be given over to the address, with picture or message (or both) restricted to the other. Inevitably it took a while for old stocks to be sold off and for the change to be completed, so it is perhaps safer to assume that the switch from undivided backs took a year or so. Once the back had been divided, it was common for 'Communication' to be printed at the top of the left hand section and 'Address' at the top to the right. On earlier divided examples, when the revised regulations were still something of a novelty, a fuller explanation often appeared on the left, such as, 'For Inland Postage ONLY, this space may now be used for communications'. The presence of such directions may suggest a date in the years immediately following the change, though allowance should again be made for old stock taking some time to sell out before new cards with a simpler heading were printed. In practice, cards as late as 1905 can be found with 'now' still included in the wording, and cards as early as 1904 can be found where the 'now' has been dropped. Broadly speaking, cards including 'now' in the formula are likely to indicate the period from 1902 to 1905/6, while a reference to 'inland postage only', without the 'now', might suggest the years 1904 to 1907. By 1907 it was possible for the back to be shared between message and address on some overseas postcards as well as on those to inland destinations. As a result instructions either became more complicated (specifying additional parts of the world) or simpler (with mention of permissible destinations being omitted entirely). Cards falling into the former category continued in use for a few years, so dating them to between 1907 and, say, 1910 would seem fair. Examples of the second type, where no mention is made of postal regulations, could come from any time after 1907.

If a card was posted, the postmark (if legible) will give a precise date for the event — though the image itself may well have been made at an earlier date. Some topographical subjects continued to be reproduced for many years. One view by Roger Fenton, who died in 1869, was reportedly still in postcard use as late as 1970. The chances, however, of someone sending a seriously out-of-date portrait must (except in cases of marked vanity) be fairly slim.

If the postmark cannot be made out, at least the monarch — Victoria, or, far more probably, one of her successors — will give some indication of date. Edward VII came to the throne in 1901, George V in 1910, Edward VIII in 1935, George VI in 1936 and Elizabeth II in 1952. But the value of the stamp can also be revealing. Before 3rd June 1918 the inland postal rate for postcards was a halfpenny (½d). From June 3rd 1918 to 12th June 1921 it was a penny (1d). From 13th June 1921 to 23rd May 1922 the price rose to 1½d, but then dropped again on 24th May 1922 to 1d. Monarch and value, taken together, can sometimes narrow the time-scale quite usefully. Thus, a George V ½d stamp dates a postcard to the period 1910 to 1918. After June 1918, incidentally, increased prices of both postage and product brought about a reduction in the frequency of postcard communication. This did not end the popularity of the postcard format for portraits, but fewer examples went through the postal system.

Nevertheless, for the sake the occasional light that might be shed, mention should be made of the changing colours of stamps. They can introduce a further stage of refinement to dating attempts. In 1900 a blue-green ½d stamp was introduced to replace the earlier orange version. Bright blue Victorian ½d stamps date from the very beginning of the blue-green issue, when difficulties were experienced with the printing ink. The first Edward VII ½d stamps, also blue-green, appeared in January 1902. Those dating from November 1904 and after were rather more yellowish-green. George V ½d stamps first appeared in 1911, and they were printed in slightly (but unhelpfully) varying shades of green throughout his reign. Green was also used for the Edward VIII ½d stamps of 1936 and the George VI versions that came out in 1937. It was not until 1950 that the ½d colour of choice was changed to orange. Stamps of higher denominations prove less helpful. Penny stamps were scarlet from before their first postcard use in 1918 until they were changed in 1952 to light ultramarine; 1½d stamps were, for their brief postcard use and longer, brown.

The determined investigator could pick up further dating hints from a close examination of the designs against which the monarch's head was set, and details of such changes may be found in any Stanley Gibbons catalogue that covers British stamps. (Most libraries should have a copy, and the edition will not be crucial, since the concern is not with recent issues.)

Even if the card was not sent by post — and many portraits in postcard format were never intended to be — it was common for the space for a stamp to be indicated on the top right-hand corner. In this space, at least during the early years of the century, the value of the required stamp was often printed.

One final aid to dating British postcards comes in the form of a free gift. The format was very popular with seaside photographers in the years between the wars, and their pier and promenade shots were often presented with the year and the name of the resort printed as part of a decorative border to the photograph.

Since families commonly spread beyond the UK's shores, and since the New World was a frequent destination, some brief mention might be made of dating postcards from the United States. Though picture cards had passed through the US post since the 1870s, it was not until 1907 that the divided back was authorised. An indication that a postcard dates from early in the divided back period is the provision of a small space for the sender's name and address. For some years there was a tendency for the picture to extend to the very edge of the card, but from around 1915 white borders were usual. Scalloped, wavy or otherwise fancy edges became popular in the 1950s. The US inland postal rate for cards was 1 cent for the first half of the century and more, except for brief 2-cent interludes from November 1917 to July 1919 and from April 1925 to June 1928.

Dating the Artefact — Transparent Images

There is something a little arbitrary about grouping such different items as slides, negatives and home movies under one heading, but they are not prints and they do have transparency in common.

Slides

In the first half of the century, slides were used primarily for entertainment and instruction, and there is no great probability that they will bear images of ancestors. Any that have survived will, like the stereographic photographs that the Victorians so enjoyed, be evidence of the family's way of life, pastimes and tastes, rather than a record of its members. But that will not prevent such pictures from being treasured items.

The standard size of early slides was 3¼ inches (8.3 cm) square, and examples of these were produced until about 1950. At first they were made of glass, and not until 1926 did celluloid examples appear. For a few years both materials were in use side-by-side, and it was only from the mid-1930s that celluloid was the standard choice.

Whilst it was quite common to colour early slides by hand, the first slides with built-in colour were made by the Autochrome process. They are characterised by their muted tones. They also often have a spotty appearance, resulting from a clumping of the starch grains that the process used as colour filters. Autochrome was launched in 1907 and faded from the scene in the 1930s. The occasional late example from the 1940s may be found.

Though the 3¼-inch slide was not yet at the end of its commercial life, an important new stage of development came with the introduction of Kodachrome transparency films in 1936. The exposed film had to be returned to the manufacturer for processing and, initially, the transparencies were returned as a strip of film to be cut up and mounted by the customer. But from 1938, they were sent back already framed in mounts that were 2 inches (5cm) square.

Since mounting and packaging provided manufacturers with opportunities for promoting their names, it is worth noting when new brands of colour transparency film appeared on the market. Agfacolor was introduced in 1936, Ansco-color in 1942, and Kodak Ektachrome in 1946. The first of these was German and the other two were American, so their impact on the UK market was not immediate, but Ektachrome film was manufactured in Britain from the early 1950s. Ilfochrome slide film also appeared in the early 1950s, and Fujicolor materials were available from 1958.

In was at the end of the 1950s that the use of colour transparency film started to become widespread in the UK.

Negatives

Attention is needed to negatives for two reasons: some have survived and may be as datable as the images they bear; others were used for contact prints that have survived, and their measurements can add help toward dating. In either case, the possible time span may be broad, but dating conclusions are often reached via an accumulation of approximations rather than from one narrowly focused clue.

Glass negatives could date from the 19th or the 20th century, and it will be the image, if anything, which indicates which side of 1900 they should be assigned to. They result from the gelatin dry plate process, which was introduced in the 1870s, and — unless they are the legacy of a professional studio practitioner — they will be the fruits of serious amateur labour. Though gelatin dry plates were still being produced in small numbers in the 1950s, such late use was confined to enthusiasts of a very dedicated kind. Surviving examples are most likely to date from the years up to and including the First World War.

Celluloid negatives can be divided according to their willingness to burn. The earlier kind, cellulose nitrate (or nitro-cellulose) proved highly inflammable. Used for motion picture stock as well as for still films, cellulose nitrate proved particularly unpredictable when tightly encased. This made the closely packed and sealed reels of early cinema film especially vulnerable. Mishaps included the destruction at Svenska, in 1941, of 95 per cent of Sweden's national film archive, when 34 years' work went up in flames in a few minutes.

Cellulose acetate 'safety' film was first tried in the early 1930s. But development and acceptance were slow, and it was not until about 1950 that acetate film completely replaced its unstable predecessor. Celluloid negatives may therefore be classed as pre-1950 or post-1930 (with a shifting balance of probabilities during the period of overlap) as long as their composition can be identified. This is not difficult, providing that a sliver of celluloid can be sacrificed: a thin shaving cut from the border of an old negative will readily produce a satisfying flare-up, whereas safety film is distinctly reluctant to catch fire. It might be added that polyester film, developed in the late 1950s, and widely used from the mid-1960s, is similarly difficult to ignite and is also resistant to tearing.

One kind of cellulose nitrate negative that can be readily recognizable is that which originates from Autographic film. This was used in some Kodak cameras, in which a small flap was opened and a metal stylus used to write details of date or subject on the backing paper. When the film was developed, the inscription appeared as black lettering on the narrow strip between images. So a negative with writing processed into the border dates from the years 1914 (when suitable cameras were first produced) to 1933 (when the specially backed film was discontinued).

The problems of dating photographs by their measurements have already been mentioned. Life is complicated by the growing use of enlargers and by the practice of fitting two negatives into an area of film that originally held one. Nevertheless, where a negative has survived, or where it seems likely that a print has been made directly from one without the intervention of an enlarger, consideration of size may be useful. Some observations on this subject were made when roll film prints were considered, and rather more systematic treatment of negative size will be found amongst the dating charts. Discussion at this point, therefore, is confined to three issues of a more general kind.

When considering the period of time in which a film size was current, it is the earliest possible date that should be regarded as more reliable. The latest date is often hard to establish. When a manufacturer ceased production of a camera that had used a new film size, owners did not suddenly throw away their old equipment. A market for the appropriate film continued for as long as enough customers made production worthwhile. Moreover, new cameras on the market might be designed for use with an existing film, and could therefore prolong its useful life.

It is also worth bearing in mind that, especially from the 1930s on, cameras were launched that could take more (and, therefore, smaller) pictures on an existing size of film. So if an image fails to coincide with any known size, it may be worth trying a piece of intelligent guesswork: double the measurement of the shorter side of the image and see if that turns the dimensions into something just under a known size. ('Just under' allows for the extra dividing border between images.)

Finally, this seems as suitable a point as any to explain the form in which sizes generally appear in this book. Measurements are usually first given in inches, with a metric equivalent following in brackets. This is because, for most of the 20th century (and certainly during its first half), imperial measurements prevailed. Formats were generally thought of in terms of inches, and the version given in centimetres is, in effect, a modern translation (and may be accurate only to the nearest millimetre). Even in the early years of the 21st century, in fact, it is still common to refer to photographic prints in imperial terms. Take in a film to a UK chemist's shop or a high street processor, and you are likely to be offered pictures of 4 x 6 inches as standard, or 5 x 7 inches as an optional but more expensive luxury. This applies even if you are handing over a strictly metric 35mm film.

Home movies
For many of us, our own moving pictures had to wait until the advent of videotape. But some families included an early amateur cinematographer whose work has, at least in part, survived. If this film has not yet been professionally transferred to videotape or disc, it probably should be, before it disintegrates completely. Meanwhile, however, it may be possible to assign some sort of date to it, to add to the evidence its images offer. As with negatives, it is dimensions that often provide such clues as are to be had — and, in the case of moving pictures, it is metric measurements that are standard. What follows, therefore, is a brief account of the origins of the moving picture and the rise of the home movie.

In 1878 Eadweard Muybridge published the first results of his attempts to break down the movement of a galloping horse into a series of still photographs. He achieved these by arranging for the horse to set off a series of cameras as it passed. In his earliest experiments exposures were triggered by threads being broken, one after another; but these soon gave way to the use of electrical signals. Photographic investigation of the movement of other animals (including birds and humans) followed, and in 1879 Muybridge unveiled the zoopraxiscope to an impressed world. This projector, by throwing a sequence of separate but consecutive images onto a screen, gave the impression of movement. Many of us, as children, drew a series of matchstick men — each a little different from the last — on the corners of exercise book pages. When we flicked through the book to see the animated results, we were employing Muybridge's principle. Because our efforts could not be projected onto a large screen, they were suitable only for private rather than public entertainment. This may well have been a good thing. Muybridge's images, however, were of considerable public interest, and since they could be copied in silhouette form onto a revolving glass disc, they could be used in a zoopraxiscope to illustrate lectures to dramatic effect.

But a revolving disc could only accommodate a simple action sequence that was repeated over and again. For any sustained narrative effect, the images needed to be on a long strip rather than a disc, and that required celluloid rather than glass. It took Eastman's 1889 introduction of celluloid roll film for still photographs to provide a kind of film material that could also be used for moving pictures. It was the brothers Auguste and Louis Lumière who turned possibility into reality: in 1895, using celluloid film in 35mm (1⅜ inches) format, they were the first to project a film in public.

The development of the cinema can be followed from this point through early documentary and narrative films, via the 1908 establishment of a film-making community in the conveniently sunny Los Angeles area, and on eventually to the present day. But commercial cinematography was not the only line to descend from Muybridge and the Lumières. Still photography had always been open to the amateur as well as to the professional — albeit, for many years, to only the well-heeled amateur. Motion photography was to be no different, and it has been suggested that the first home movie was a Russian film of Cossack horsemen, made in 1896. In 1912, only four years after the founding of Hollywood, Charles Pathé introduced the KOK home cinematograph. It used 28mm (1⅛ inches) cellulose acetate safety film and was the first moving-picture system aimed at the domestic user. Most projector owners, however, used the equipment to show bought films rather than films they had made themselves.

The real opening up of amateur creativity came in the 1920s. Pathé's 9.5mm (⅜ inch) safety film, with accompanying equipment, came onto the market in 1922. This brought moving pictures within the reach of a much wider public. Then, in 1923, the Cine-Kodak Motion Picture Camera and Kodascope projector, using 16mm (⅝ inch) safety film, proved sufficiently popular for a network of Kodak processing laboratories to grow up across the world. The same year saw the creation of Britain's first amateur cinematograph club at Cambridge University. The first colour film for amateur use, also in 16mm format, followed in 1928.

It was an enthusiastic start, but the enthusiasm could only be exercised by those who had money to spare. It was the arrival of 8mm (just under ⅜ inch) cameras and films in 1932 that created increasing competition in the home movie market. Competition led to an easing of prices, and as a result the moving equivalent of the holiday snap became an option for a greater percentage of the population. Though equipment and materials were not particularly cheap – and were certainly rarely aspired to by the working classes – a middle class or professional level of affluence could offer entry to this exciting world.

The amateur filmmaker at this stage was, characteristically, a serious hobbyist and, very probably, a club member. Competitions were popular. Some keen entrants directed their own dramas, but most simply recorded outings, family holidays and local events. Though colour had been available since 1928, it was Kodak's tri-pack movie film (issued in 16mm format in 1935, and in 8mm format in 1936) that first brought a degree of popularity to filming in colour.

Sound also became an option for the enthusiast of the 1930s, but it was not much taken up before the war. Afterwards a moneyed few went in for sound, but the rise of television in the 1950s rather inhibited its possibilities for further growth.

Nevertheless, inasmuch as there was ever a boom in home movies, it started after the Second World War and was over by the mid-60s. By then the activity had become largely one for the aspiring cinéaste, rather than for the taker of moving snapshots.

From the second half of the 1940s, 8mm became the standard gauge for amateur use, and it was given a boost by Kodak's introduction of better quality Super 8 film in 1965. The market share for 9.5mm film slowly declined during these years (though it did not disappear entirely until around 1980). The 16mm format continued to find devotees, especially among those with artistic pretensions.

From the middle of the 1960s, the home cinema struggled against the competition of television. The excitement of seeing your own moving images in the living room dwindled in the face of seeing somebody else's images — especially since that somebody else made a rather more polished product and offered something different every night. Kodak's launch, in 1974, of a cartridge version of Super 8 may have had the ability to revitalise business, but by then electronic video-recording systems were making their first, hesitant inroads into the market.

Dating the Image – Pose and Action

Studio photographs

The Victorian age had seen the professional camera coming closer to the subject over the years, from the full-length shots of the 1860s to the head-and-shoulder or even head-and-collar vignettes of the 1890s. Such vignettes — with a round or oval close-up fading away into whiteness at the edges — were still sometimes chosen for early Edwardian pictures, and they were especially popular for such cabinet prints as were still being produced. But this effect, which had come close to monopolising the family albums of the 1890s, now quickly lost its firm hold on photographic fashion. The camera moved back, and full-length (or near full-length) shots of both seated and standing subjects became common again. The feet were often included, though sometimes there was a cut-off line at around calf level. These long shots remained popular for the first 20 or so years of the century, and still found some favour thereafter, especially where two or more people were being fitted into the space.

Poses and expressions at first retained something of the formality associated with Victorian portraits. Uncomfortably long exposures were by and large a thing of the past, (though occasional photographers resolutely resisted electric studio lighting for ten or even more years of the new century). But dignity in photographs had not simply been the by-product of long exposures. The Victorians had believed in dignity, and, in the studio at least, the Edwardians did not readily give it up. Nevertheless, there is often something a little more relaxed about portraits in the period before the First World War. Subjects often contrive to look calmly respectable without seeming either grim or uncomfortable. This can be particularly noticeable in photographs of young women, who retain the traditional cool composure, but who return the camera's stare with a directness and confidence that was not always evident in the pictures of their mothers.

As the 1920s progressed, a taste grew for shots that showed head and shoulders or upper body, and this persisted through the 1930s. A closer attention to the face was often accompanied by an apparent consciousness of overall effect on the part of the photographer or the subject (or, quite possibly, both). Some sense of photography as art was filtering from the worlds of fashion and film into the visual vocabulary of popular portraiture. Edward Steichen, for instance, who was a prominent photographer for fashion magazines of the 1920s, had a curriculum vitae that stretched back to the artistic values of the Photo-Secession movement and in 1905 had worked with its founder, Alfred Steiglitz, to establish a gallery in New York. Influential, too, were Man Ray's stylised and impassive portraits of members of 1920s Parisian society. This does not mean that the average studio practitioner was trying to emulate the work of specific individuals. But it does suggest, in very broad terms, that the provincial professionals were working to keep up with their more glamorous colleagues.

A symptom of this changing vision, as the 1920s unfolded, was a tendency to stress the streamlined and the athletic, with subjects seeming more lithe and stylish than their stolid predecessors. (Costume, of course, played its part in this effect). But there was also a sense of control, which distinguished the professional product from the exuberance so often shown in amateur pictures. One way of achieving this was the posing of the sitter in low relief with limbs kept in the same plane and legs crossed. Or the lower half of the body might be turned sideways on, while head and (perhaps) shoulders were twisted towards the camera. The careful deployment of limbs could be enhanced by draping an arm along the back of a chair.

In practice, the more dramatic versions of such effects might be a little contrived for a run-of-the-mill family photograph. Attention to the positioning of the subject can, nevertheless, frequently be seen in an angling of the body and a turning of the head. Even the Victorians did not always present themselves square-on to the camera, and Edwardian photos show a higher incidence of sitters viewed at a slight angle. But the 1920s saw a more determined avoidance of the full-faced military stance, and there was widespread acceptance of the notion that head and chest need not always point in the same direction.

Once varied angles of head and body became commonplace, varied angles of lighting followed. A portrait still needed to show the features clearly, but a moderate amount of shadow on the far side of a half-turned face could add atmosphere without sacrificing a sense of identity. (The cynic might argue that the photographers of the 1920s were merely rediscovering conventions of posing and lighting that had been familiar to such as David Wilkie Winfield and Julia Margaret Cameron some half century before.)

At the same time, and on into the 1930s, the influence of the cinema was becoming stronger and shaping people's feelings about how they wished to appear. Men may have entertained their own fantasies about film-star looks, but it is in portraits of women that the spirit of Hollywood is most likely to be discerned. In general terms, it may be seen in the use of soft focus, in strong contrasts of light and shade, and perhaps in the use of backlighting to define the hair and create an aura. The serious student of film may be able to decide which performer is being flattered by imitation. (Are we confronted with the wistful pallor and long white throat of a Lillian Gish, or with the blonde waved hair, half-closed eyes and petulant mouth of a Jean Harlow?) It was quite possible, though, for elements of different actresses' images to be combined in the attempt to look alluring. Most researchers will therefore settle for an approximate date of 30s or late 20s, rather than try to connect a portrait with the way a particular performer looked in a particular film distributed in a particular year.

People continued to adopt the style and manner of popular entertainers after the 1930s. In fact, they have probably never stopped — though opportunities for self-absorption were perhaps rather limited during the Second World War and the years of austerity that immediately followed it. But the number of commercial practitioners was dwindling, and the opportunities for romantic portraits were becoming fewer. Professional pictures of returned servicemen reunited with their families were quite common in the second half of the 1940s, and the tradition survived of going to the studio to mark major family milestones and events. But in the second half of the century the professionals spent more time outside the studio, attending not only weddings but also schools, graduations and department store promotions. Their pictures served a purpose and (the occasional soft-focus wedding photo aside) the making of a clear, well-lit record was often more important than the creation of mood or drama.

Roll film photographs

While all these shifts of fashion and practice were taking place, hordes of amateurs, most of them equipped with simple but effective box cameras, were taking pictures too.

Their photographs were taken out of doors, since that is where sufficient light could be found, and they quickly acquired their own set of conventions. A degree of relaxation came into the picture, and people in photographs even started to smile. The photographer was generally a friend or relative, and that could help to ease the situation. The outdoor setting also played its part, for sitting in the garden or taking a country walk are more liberating experiences than sitting in a studio. Then there was the fact that exposure times were shorter than in the past. This meant that expressions no longer had to be planned and held; a spontaneous response to the camera could be captured on film. Finally, values were changing. Whilst the desire for respectability was not jettisoned, a degree of informality and cheerfulness did not seem objectionable. Indeed, since much snapshooting took place on outings — during which the intention was to have a good time — smiling seemed quite appropriate. All of these factors combined to deliver a new message. Broadly speaking, the 19th century photograph had said, 'Look, I'm respectable.' Its 20th century amateur counterpart, on the other hand, said, 'Look, I'm happy.'

Whilst amateur posing or grouping of subjects does not, in itself, provide sufficient argument for dating, some general trends may be picked out for adding to other evidence.

Characteristic roll film subjects in the years leading up to the First World War included people standing, individually or in groups, at the threshold of the house. The family home was a natural enough subject to record, and the front door was usually as close to the inside of it as light conditions allowed the camera to come. People also took some pride in the entrance to their houses, whitening steps, setting them off with pot plants, or growing climbing plants beside and over the door. So the threshold provided a suitable setting where members of the family might proudly stand, and such scenes were very popular in the Edwardian years. Since the garden was an extension of the home, that also figured in many snaps, and pictures of people assembled in the yard or taking tea on the lawn are not uncommon.

Pictures were also taken further afield, for the new box cameras were highly portable, and country-walk photos were typical of the pre-war years. People paused during excursions to have their pictures taken. Mounds and slopes were useful for reclining on, trees were good for leaning against, and stiles and fences provided handy perches. All could provide a focal point around which to organise a group. This use of countryside features for support or composition played its own part in creating the informality of the roll-film picture: it is hard to sprawl on a bank or balance on a stile whilst summoning up the gravitas that can be projected from a substantial studio chair. It will be noticed, however, that countryside shots, like garden pictures, were still rather static.

People were most frequently shown at full length, and sometimes at an unnecessary distance. Feet were generally in view and so, often, was quite a lot of foreground. This characteristic of the snapshooter's work (which has never entirely disappeared) owes much to the fear of 'not getting everything in'. Faced with the possibility of inadvertently scalping subjects or of cutting out people on the edge of a group, the nervous amateur plays safe by allowing a little room for error. It was a very understandable precaution in the early days of do-it-yourself photography, since the very first popular cameras had no viewfinders. Guided by the 'V' marked on top of the box, the operator simply pointed the device in the desired direction and hoped for the best. The snap-photographer's diffidence did not, however, die out when cameras became more sophisticated — as many family albums will bear witness.

Whilst pictures of subjects standing or sitting still continued to be the most usual, more active shots were tried in the years between the wars. Encouraged perhaps by growing confidence, by more reliable equipment and by the professional ploy of snatching shots as potential customers passed along the promenade, amateur photographers now recorded their subjects walking in the country, at the seaside and along the street. The 1920s and, more particularly, the 1930s were the age of people striding out in photos.

Cycling was another activity that found its way into the family collection, though the faster movement involved meant that owners were generally posed on their machines rather than caught in the act of pedalling. On roads that were still uncongested, cycling became a very popular pastime, and it reached its peak (in both the doing and the depicting) in the 1930s.

The period between world wars also saw the rise of a kind of fabricated photographic jollity. People wanted to prove that they felt at ease in front of the lens. They were, perhaps, keen to demonstrate the values of the age by showing that they were happy. So they larked and joked for the camera, projecting hilarity, flinging their arms around each other, riding on each other's backs or adopting pseudo-dramatic poses. Such jocund self-consciousness is very occasionally found in Victorian studio photographs of young men, and it can also be seen in some early roll-film pictures. But it is very limited, and women are unlikely to be found joining in – at least until the dressing up that accompanied the 1919 peace celebrations. The rise of the jokey photograph belongs most firmly to the 1920s and 1930s.

One further before-camera activity of this period needs some comment. As soon as the camera moved out of doors, it started to record people smoking. The figure standing with cigarette in hand became a common feature of photographs in the years preceding the First World War. But, for some time, that figure was nearly always male. It took quite a while for women smoking in public to become acceptable. (In 1904, a woman in New York was arrested for doing so.) By the second half of the 1920s, however, women in photographs are more frequently seen holding cigarettes, and the business of lighting up can even be used as the focal point for the composition of a small group.

After the Second War the common conventions of amateur snapshots continued. Photographers stood further from their subjects than they needed to, and subjects played the fool for the benefit of photographers. But, especially during the 1950s, a greater variety and richness of repertoire developed. Children played; adults stood beside the family's first car; travellers ventured to more distant places and posed in front of the most memorable bits. Affordable flash allowed indoor pictures, and Christmas joined summer holidays on the photographic agenda. The amateur was recording life as it occurred, as well as just inviting it to pause and smile.

Dating the Image — Costume

As with the 19th century so with the 20th, people's clothes frequently offer the most obvious clues for dating photographs. Women's clothes remain easier to date than men's, since they were subject to a succession of fashions that was both more rapid and more visually striking. But a word or two of caution is necessary. The fashions of one decade could be worn long after it. This was true especially of the elderly, with their limited taste for change, and of the less affluent, who could not afford to update their wardrobe constantly. So, for example, pictures of women's group outings in the early 1920s show sprinklings of the broad, cake-shaped hats that were popular in the late Edwardian period, and pictures of hop-pickers in the 1930s are liberally laced with the cloche hats that prevailed in the previous decade. The beginning and end of a trend may seem quite clear if fashion plates are consulted, but change is likely to be less precisely defined amongst the mass of the population.

Women's clothes up to the Second World War
After the emphasis on sleeves and shoulders during the 1890s, the new century ushered in a rather sleek look. Corsetry created a heavy busted stance, while skirts fitted closely over the hips before opening out into a swirling bell shape and ending, in the more formal examples, in a train. Sleeves tended to be tight (sometimes relieved by a little puffing or fullness at the shoulder) and long (sometimes covering half the hand). There was an emphasis on curves, on tight waists, and on hems that swept the ground. Ornament could be provided by a profusion of lace and frills, while a taste for soft and light materials created a generally summery look. Bodices might be loose and billowing, perhaps trimmed to emphasise the bust before being caught back into a narrow waist. The S-shaped effect of all this could be very pronounced, though the most extreme examples belong more to fashion illustrations and high society than to everyday life.

The look was short-lived. By 1908 the S-shape was already more subdued, with the forward thrust of bosom and backward thrust of hips becoming less pronounced. Then in 1909 came the appearance of close-fitting tube-like dresses with hobble skirts, narrowed at the ankles in a way that recalled men's peg-top trousers. These skirts could seriously impede walking, and a forgetful vigorous stride could result in torn material or unladylike stumbling. So a fetter, secured at calf level, was sometimes used to keep unthinking athleticism in check.

For people of the humbler sort, the blouse and skirt combination — which had found favour in the 1890s — became even more popular. It was smart, practical and, for the New Woman, businesslike. White blouse with long, dark skirt was frequently the workwear of choice for office employees and teachers. Over the blouse a bolero jacket or an Eton bodice (which rather resembled a boy's Eton jacket) was often worn. The blouse itself had long sleeves, tight at the wrist and with cuffs that often extended over part of the hand. Whilst relatively simple and sensible blouses might be appropriate for everyday use, opportunities were also found for wearing something more frothy and elaborate. As on dresses, lace or the less expensive Irish crochet might be liberally added to soft fabric to achieve a light and summery effect. Until about 1908 it was usual for the blouse to hang loosely over the waist at the front. But then, in a change that reflected the new fashion in dress styles, this floppiness quickly disappeared.

The rather plain skirts that accompanied the blouses tended to be full in both length and cut. Tight at the waist and smooth over the hips, they flared out below, and gores were sometimes introduced to give them additional substance. Extra trimmings were generally reserved for the upper part of the body.

Hair in the early 1900s was generally dressed high on the head, though loops and coils at the back (teapot-handle or doorknocker styles left over from the 1890s) were still sometimes to be seen. Pads were often used to build up the volume of the hair, and these were very useful for sticking in the pins needed to secure large hats.

These hats are often the most striking feature of later Edwardian and early Georgian photographs. Franz Lehar's operetta, *The Merry Widow*, played a major part in establishing their ubiquity. Previewed in Vienna in 1905, it inspired a fashion that swept Europe: big hats became the order of the day. They could be tall, and they could be heavily trimmed. Feathers were a particularly popular form of decoration, and the ostrich served Edwardian society well, providing for boas as well as headgear. But, above all, it was the width of brim that counted, and the characteristic shape of such a hat was that of a gateau on a large plate. It was a style that dominated from around 1908, and though there was some shift to smaller hats just before the First World War, examples of the gateau-style are still to be found in post-war photographs.

The rise of the broad-brimmed hat coincided with the arrival of the hobble skirt and created a new silhouette. If the woman of fashion began Edward VIII's reign looking like the letter S, she ended it looking like a tall, inverted triangle. Just before and after 1910, her hat might be wider than the hips that tapered down to tottering fettered ankles. It was a shape that provoked some amusement, and it is not really surprising that humorists compared it to that of a clothes peg. (The current effectiveness of this comparison does, however, rely on an ability to remember the old-fashioned, one-piece, wooden clothes peg rather than the later spring-loaded variety.)

Light opera was not the only art to have an influence on fashion in the pre-war years. Dance made a contribution, too. Diaghilev's Ballets Russes visited Paris in 1909, and Léon Bakst's designs, especially those for *Schéhérazade* and *Cléopâtre*, caused a sensation. The result was a European wave of orientalism, with such real or supposed Eastern ingredients as bright silks, brocades, feathers in the hair, kimonos, turbans, and ropes of beads or pearls hung around the bodice. It was a taste for the exotic that was perhaps mainly expressed by the most fashionable, but it also played its part in the general softening of drapery and narrowing of skirts that occurred between 1910 and 1914.

There were several fashion developments in the years immediately preceding the First World War. One of them affected that well-established favourite, the blouse. In 1913, the V-neck suddenly appeared on the scene. The effect was really quite restrained and unrevealing, but severe moralists were scandalised. Some doctors, too, were alarmed. They argued that such scanty attire exposed the wearer to the elements and constituted a threat to health. They therefore condemned the new garments as 'pneumonia blouses'.

Nevertheless, the V-neck blouse was widely adopted and very quickly became widespread.

The V-neck, often with a modesty panel inserted, was also a feature of the high-waisted Empire line, another favourite of these years. Other fashion details to emerge just before the war included the knee-length overskirt and smaller hats. These hats fitted closely to the head, but often bore a feather or two sticking jauntily out or up. On dresses and blouses, buttons were supplanting lace as the favourite form of decoration.

War brought with it a need for rather more practical clothes. Skirts became fuller again and, gradually, a little shorter. By the close of the war they ended above the ankle (but still below the calf) and were quite likely to be accompanied by boots. Clothes were often tailor-made, with an emphasis on the sensible rather than the fashionable. Some women went in for suits. Others preferred tunic-like bodices that fell over the top of the skirt and ended at around the level of mid-thigh.

The pale colours that had been so popular gave way, to an extent, to rather more sombre hues. Where they survived, they were used less demonstratively — as in the simple white cotton dresses that gained some acceptance across all classes of society. The white blouse also remained on the scene, often in a plain form that amounted to a shirt and that was sometimes set off by a tie. It provided a natural adjunct to the suit.

There also appeared an alternative to the traditional blouse. It was the 'jumper blouse', made without front opening or buttons, and loose enough to be slipped over the head. It could then be held at the waist with a sash.

Some styles were influenced by the hostilities. Women's first excursion into trousers and breeches came when, to aid the war effort, they took up work in factories and on the land. For the time being, however, such garments remained purely occupational wear in strictly limited circumstances. Less restricted was the adoption of outdoor coats that were modelled on the soldier's trench-coat, and that featured large pockets, leather buttons and belts.

By the end of the war, certain aspects of 1920s style were already being prefigured. Though wide-brimmed hats remained in evidence, narrow-brimmed and brimless hats had become quite become common during the war; and though the highly fashionable flirted briefly with bicorn and tricorn designs, head-hugging hats were widespread by 1919. Waistlines, too, were changing. By about 1918 they had dropped to somewhere just above the hip — a move away from the tight waist for which both the tunic bodice and the jumper blouse might be considered precedents.

The fashions of the 1920s may be seen as reflecting a post-war optimism in a younger generation that was anxious to make up for lost time. For women, this meant a reaction against stiff corsets, cumbersome skirt lengths and voluminous petticoats. It was an age that took frivolity seriously, making its point by way of heavy indulgence in costume jewellery, fringed trimmings and swinging beads. So strong may be the sense of levity that the modern eye can even have difficulty in discerning an outfit's purpose, finding it hard to distinguish daywear from sportswear or even night attire.

The stereotypical 1920s young woman had a boyish look, with flattened bosom, short skirt and waistline set at the hip. Her hair was smooth, short, and covered by a cloche hat. But a little more detail than that is both possible and helpful.

The long, tubular 'barrel line' skirt first appeared in 1919 and, combined with the dropped waistline, laid the foundation for the slim, straight outline of the age. Some women helped the impression along by using chest flatteners. But this effect of parallel verticals was not immediately universal. For the first few years of the 1920s, some women wore skirts that flared out from the hip-level waist, and a taste for pleats undermined the appearance of uniformity. Nevertheless, it was the straight-up-and-down style that prevailed. Women looked boyish — or even mannish, if they chose to finish off their ensemble with bow tie and masculine-looking jacket and hat.

Then, in around 1924 or 1925, the short skirt made its shocking appearance. Ending at the knee or just a little lower, it provoked outrage. Some US states attempted to introduce a legal ban on such immodesty, and an Italian prelate believed that these garments were calling down the wrath of God. But the decade's dominant look was not to be compromised. The 'garçonne' style won the day, curves were out, and hemlines were high. Dresses tended to be shift-like and simple, while unfussy necklines and collarless jackets, worn in conjunction with short hair, emphasised the throat. In photographs from the 1920s you notice women's necks in a way that just doesn't happen with earlier or later pictures.

Fashion is rarely, if ever, democratic or kind, and the boyish outline was more easily achieved by some women than by others. But the basic lines of 1920s clothes tend to be discernible, however successfully or unsuccessfully they are being worn. There are, too, features other than dress shape and skirt length to be looked for.

Bold, printed textiles were popular, and light or diaphanous fabrics — such as silk, rayon and organza — were frequently chosen. After the 1922 discovery of Tutankhamun's tomb, Egyptian motifs became quite the thing, and Chinese designs also received an enthusiastic response. Some liking for pleated skirts continued through the decade, and sleeves were often wide. In 1926 the 'little black dress' became fashionable and was often worn long, almost reaching the ankles. The second half of the decade also saw the appearance of hemlines that were curved or angled to look uneven, and scalloped hems became fashionable at its end.

Much use was made of accessories. Beads and bracelets, ropes of pearls and scarves were all popular, and eye-catching shoes with assertive buckles and T-shaped straps were much in vogue. Silk stockings were highly characteristic of the time, (and their sheen makes them readily identifiable in photographs). Nail varnish made its appearance. But in especial need of attention are the adornments relating to the head.

Whilst wide-brimmed hats were slow to disappear, particularly amongst the older generation, it was the cloche hat that, perhaps more than anything else, became the symbol of the 1920s. The cloche was, in effect, a tall, often slightly bulbous dome of fabric pulled well down onto the head, which it fitted snugly. It often lacked a brim, though small-brimmed derivatives are also seen in photographs. The younger sort wore the cloche with the short-skirted shift, while their elders wore it to accompany rather staid versions of the low-waisted line. It was considered stylish, and it also had its more practical aspects: jammed down over the ears, it was very suitable for motoring; and, in my own family at least, it proved an invaluable accessory for seasick Girl Guides. It was one of those items which (like flared trousers) make people blush with embarrassment when viewing snaps of their younger selves, but which seemed, at the time, both enchanting and indispensable. Towards the end of the decade there appeared a form of cloche that was longer at the back than at the front. Its shape rather suggested a coal-scuttle.

Even when headgear other than the cloche was worn, it seemed to pay homage to the prevailing style. Broad headbands and scarves tied into tight turbans echoed the cloche both in their closeness to the head and in their drawing of a horizontal line across the brow. Sun hats had very broad brims, but their round crowns echoed the familiar cloche shape.

Hairstyles were well suited to the hats they bore. In the early 1920s the bob became fashionable. This complemented the popular boyish look, for the hair was worn fairly short and close to the head, rather like a helmet. The style was typified by actress Louise Brooks, whose smooth dark hair (with straight fringe and side pieces curving down over the temples) was much imitated. By the time of her most notable success in G. W. Pabst's *Pandora's Box* (1928), however, some of her contemporaries had already moved on. For the really enthusiastic follower of fashion, the shingle brought in a sleeker style that was cut to highlight the shape of the back of the head, while 1927 saw the introduction of the even shorter and more boyish Eton crop.

The face beneath the hair also underwent a change during the decade, as it became acceptable for the use of make-up to be discernible. Indeed, no very acute powers of observation are needed to notice the plucked and arched brows and cupid-bow lips that are sometimes evident in photographs dating from this period.

Towards the end of the 1920s softer dress and skirt shapes began to emerge and to cling more closely to the figure. New hairstyles, too, were heralded, as Marcel Grateau pioneered the first successful artificial waves. A return to femininity was beginning and would underlie the look of the 1930s.

The change in style occurred quite quickly. The shock of the 1929 Wall Street crash was felt far beyond the United States, and the world became a more sober place. As far as fashion was concerned, this did not mean that women underwent a sudden conversion to sackcloth and ashes. But it did involve a return to the security of conventions. A more traditionally feminine look returned: hemlines dropped, the waist returned to its original place, and hair was grown again.

A new fashionable shape emerged, focusing on width of shoulder and slenderness of hips. Dresses were slim and straight, bodices were softly draped, waists were redefined, and skirts ended below the knee. Height was admired, so there was a tendency to emphasise the vertical. Attention to shoulders and sleeves was common. Breadth of shoulder could partly be achieved in the cutting of garments, and padding frequently reinforced the impression. Dresses incorporating capes or featuring short, frilled 'butterfly' sleeves drew attention to shoulders and upper arms, and 1933 saw a modest revival of the leg-of-mutton sleeve for evening wear. This style, which had been much in vogue in the mid-1890s, contrasted a closely wrapped lower arm with a ballooning-out of fabric from elbow to shoulder. Less dramatic (but possibly more popular) was the 'bishop' sleeve, billowing loosely down the arm from the shoulder before becoming tight at the wrist.

Suits came back into favour for women. Sharply tailored in a way that the 'power dressing' of the 1980s was later to echo, they gave an air of chic efficiency. Lapels were often wide, echoing the width of the shoulders. For more casual occasions on the other hand, trousers now made an appearance and gained limited acceptance. Usually designed with wide and rather baggy legs, they sometimes served as leisurewear and, at the seaside, took the form of beach pyjamas.

Fur had made some appearance for trimming clothes in the 1920s. But it was in the 1930s that an enthusiasm for fur really took off. It was still used as a trimming, but it also achieved the status of a fabric in its own right. Fur wraps and fur coats became common. They were to remain objects of desire, mainly at the expensive end of the market, until at least the 1950s, (after which fake fur and conscience combined to erode their perceived glamour). But in the 1930s, the wearing of fur was not especially remarkable. Mink and ermine might have been too costly, but fox and rabbit were relatively affordable. Fox furs were particularly popular, and a complete pelt – with head and tail intact and worn as a stole – was a badge of respectable middle age well into the 1940s.

On the legs, silk stockings were still being worn. But by now there had been some success in the development of synthetic fabrics, and nylons had appeared on the scene. On the feet, open-toed shoes and sandals were popular, and there was a taste for a two-toned finish to both open- and closed-toe designs.

At the other end of the body, the cloche was slow to disappear completely. But it was pushed from the limelight by other possibilities. Some women took to wearing small hats with slanted brims that could be tilted jauntily over one eye. These hats often bore a distinct resemblance to the male trilby, and this taste for headgear with a masculine air owed much to the influence of Marlene Dietrich. Other women opted for the beret, which could also be tilted to one side. But at the same time it was becoming much more acceptable for women to be seen hatless in public, and hair was being grown longer again. Still often dressed close to the head, it was organised into soft waves. There was a craze for blonde hair after Jean Harlow peroxided hers for the 1930 film, *Hell's Angels*, and there were also fads for wearing decorative combs and for folding the hair into a flower-topped chignon. As for the face, that was as much if not more subject to the plucking of eyebrows and application of make-up as it had been in the 1920s.

Then, after the age of 1920s frivolity and the era of 1930s glamour and femininity, war broke out again. Austerity accompanied it, and clothes rationing was in force from 1941 to 1949. Points were assigned to items of attire, taking into account both the nature of the garment and how much material it used. A civilian woman was allotted 66 points a year, of which two would have to be surrendered every time she bought a pair of stockings and about seven if she purchased a simple dress. It was necessary to think what was needed, rather than what was wanted. Inevitably, therefore, women had to buy carefully and to make the most of the clothes they already possessed. What is more, the film star looks of the 1930s came to seem a little flashy and lacking in the patriotic seriousness called for by the times. Value and staying power took on a new importance, and the Utility Scheme — covering such products as clothes and furniture — made government-approved goods available at fixed prices.

So plenty of clothes from the 1930s stayed in circulation, while what was new was above all, sensible. Rather square shoulders remained common for both coats and dresses. Suit-type jackets still met with approval, but they were increasingly worn with skirts of a different colour, as women found they could squeeze an extra lease of life out of their wardrobe by mixing and matching.

Flower-print fabrics had not been unknown in the 1930s, but nor had they been especially popular. Now they were very commonly used for dresses. But the floral pattern was likely to be fairly small. (Material was in short supply, and less of it was wasted in matching up small repeats at the seams.) Skirts were relatively short, settling at around knee length but cutting an inch or two off 1930s fashions. In this way, and by being fairly narrow, they used up a little less fabric.

Floral and patterned material was also used for that least glamorous of garments, the wrap-around pinafore. It had been in evidence for years — usually in plain material — as a practical item to protect the clothes it covered. It came largely into the category of occupational costume, being worn for such activities as market work and portering. But in the 1940s it became quite standard workwear around the house, and its appearance in brighter prints marked its new status.

The dressing of legs caused women some concern, not least because the fairly short skirts left a fair stretch of limb to cover. Stockings were on ration. A year's coupons, if (improbably) devoted to nothing else, would allow for a new pair about once every ten days. But stockings laddered with depressing ease. It really was what they did best. So women found themselves driven to other expedients. The fashion-conscious tried painting their legs, complete with pencilled seams, to look as if stockings were being worn. Gravy browning was reputed to be an effective colouring medium. Others (generally younger women) opted for ankle socks instead. But for some women, trousers provided the answer. They were often the most practical wear for wartime occupations, and they certainly sidestepped the stocking problem. Designs were generally fairly baggy, allowing ample freedom of movement. Finally, for the lower limbs, there was a need for shoes. These too tended to be serviceable rather than glamorous: sensible, heavy shoes wore well, and that was what mattered most.

Accessories and trimmings can, in the spirit of the age, be briefly dealt with. There was sometimes a rather military hint to belts and buttons; shoulder bags were often preferred to their hand-held equivalents; fur was still popular, especially in the form of a whole fox.

Then there was the head. Hats tilted to one side were still seen, but some wide-brimmed hats were also worn in the early years of the war. Later, a degree of adaptation and customisation went on, since new hats were not high on many shopping lists. But far more characteristic of the age were such practical coverings as headscarves and plastic rain hoods. The beret, too, was often worn — it may have been acquired back in the 1930s, but its unshowiness and its military associations made it seem attuned to the times. But it was hair rather than hats that added a little panache to a woman's appearance. Hair was now worn much longer, often down to the shoulders, and it hung in carefully manufactured waves. A little heap of permed curls was often built up on top of the head to form an attention-catching departure point from which the tresses artfully fell. Some women — influenced by film star Veronica Lake — contrived to have a lock of hair falling over one eye. The war may have denied women many opportunities for show, but through their hair they were able to express a taste for extravagance which could find no outlet elsewhere.

Men's clothes up to the Second World War

The story of men's costume is more briefly told.

Lounge suits, introduced some years earlier, had become widespread during the 1890s, and by the early 1900s they had become fairly normal daywear. Thanks to the invention of the trouser press in the mid 1890s, sharp creases in trouser legs had become quite common. Turn-ups, which had been briefly seen in the early 1890s, made a tentative reappearance in about 1902. They became popular from around 1912 and were then the standard way of ending trouser legs for many years. There was still some use of the frock coat for formal occasions.

Shirt collars were high at the beginning of the century, having reached about 3 inches at the end of the 1890s. They were starched to keep them stiffly impressive.

Whilst the top hat was the normal accompaniment to the frock coat, the soft and level-brimmed homburg hat was becoming an increasingly popular adjunct to the lounge suit. Straw boaters, which had been around since the 1870s, were now very much in vogue. The cloth cap was leading a double life. Originally it had functioned as outdoor wear with sporting overtones — a suitable companion for the belted Norfolk jacket and knickerbockers. But it came to find favour with the working man, and its two rather different social connotations existed side by side. By the time of the First World War a variety of street headgear was possible for the male civilian: homburgs, bowlers and cloth caps were all common, and top hats were still not extinct.

Military uniform is also, of course, commonly seen in photographs dating from the war years, and the tunics and calf-length puttees of this period are easily distinguished from the battle dress blouses and ankle-hugging gaiters of the Second World War.

After the war a new informality came into men's costume. Hats, gloves and waistcoats could all still be worn, but they were no longer de rigueur. Bright ties and suede shoes made their appearance, as did the two-tone footwear popularly known as 'co-respondent shoes'. Another new arrival of the 1920s — and one that was to survive at least until the 1950s — was the Fair Isle pullover, a woollen slipover in which assertive colours were worked in intricate designs. Checks and diamonds were popular, but so were mixed patterns chosen to demonstrate the knitter's versatility much in the manner of a sampler.

Double-breasted jackets came into favour in the 1920s, and there was also (in the latter part of the decade especially) some taste for double-breasted waistcoats. The waistlines of jackets tended to be clearly defined, and a folded handkerchief was often worn in the breast pocket.

Two styles of trouser belong especially to these years. The old-fashioned knickerbockers blossomed out into something rather roomier. Influenced perhaps by the fairly capacious breeches of guards' officers, they were cut loosely before being caught in at sock level. In this incarnation they were called 'plus-fours'. Full-length trousers also came to be more generously cut. These flapping, wide-legged garments were known as 'Oxford bags' and were said to originate from the very baggy trousers worn by undergraduates over their rowing shorts. The Prince of Wales adopted the style as early as 1922, and by the middle of the decade it was hugely popular. At their most determinedly fashionable, Oxford bags were so wide as to virtually conceal the feet, but such excess was not destined to last for long. Nevertheless, trouser legs remained fairly wide into and through the 1930s.

Hats were still usually worn out of doors, and a variety of styles was still possible. A group photograph might very well include a mixture of flat caps, homburgs, trilbies and bowlers. The top hat had, by now, become something for grand occasions, and the bowler was, to a degree, its successor. The trilby gained ground in the 1920s (and went on to overshadow bowler and homburg in the 1930s and 1940s). Though not entirely unlike the homburg, the trilby brought a degree of rakishness to the soft hat world: whereas the level brim of the homburg was curled up quite tightly all round, the trilby's brim curved gently at the back and sides and was pulled down at the front. The flat cap continued to straddle the social worlds. Often rather wide and baggy, it was just the thing to go with plus-fours and emanated a certain rural jauntiness. But worn with a collarless shirt and a waistcoat, it was firmly proletarian. Indeed, rolled-up shirtsleeves, dark waistcoat, no collar, flat cap and cigarette were the key ingredients of the working class off-duty look from the 1920s until the Second World War and after. (For formal occasions, such as Saturday night's visit to the pub, a collar, tie and suit jacket might be added.)

By the 1930s the cap had become the dominant headgear of the common man and was worn for both work and leisure. The bowler was still seen, but it was worn by the manager, the office worker and, perhaps, the foreman. Look at pictures of the 1936 Jarrow marchers, and you find yourself scanning a sea of flat caps.

The jackets of the 1930s tended to be relatively short, and they often had padded shoulders and wide lapels. Striped blazers were also in favour, and trouser legs were still rather wide. Shirts with soft built-in collars became quite popular, and these — if worn without tie and open at the neck — helped the younger sort to cut a dash. One popular combination was blazer, open-necked shirt and cravat. Nevertheless, ties were still commonly worn for leisure as well as for more solemn occasions.

For male as well as for female fashions the Second World War was a fairly static period, but photographs of men in uniform became common again. For soldiers the uniform had moved on, and waist-length battledress blouses were now the norm. Ankles were wrapped in strapped and buckled gaiters, over the top of which a billow of trapped trouser leg was folded (more or less neatly) down. Flat-topped, peaked caps were no longer the standard wear, and the lower ranks usually wore berets or forage caps. But men in the forces were also, unwittingly, in the vanguard of fashion, for some of their garments were to be transformed into everyday civilian wear in the 1950s: the naval duffle coat and heavy roll-neck sweater, the flying jacket that would prove invaluable to motor cyclists, and the battledress blouse that was to transmute into the windcheater.

The young

Such children's styles as had been developed by the Victorians took many years to disappear. The long-popular sailor suit (or, for girls, sailor top and skirt) was common at least until the 1920s, as was the large white shirt collar worn inside the jacket (as at Eton) or outside (as at Harrow). But, to a degree, children's clothes in the early decades of the 20th century — like those of the 19th century — tended to be smaller versions of what their elders were wearing.

Certain Victorian rites of passage also survived. Girls continued to wear their hair long until they were allowed to catch it up into an adult hairstyle at the age of about 16-18. This practice was still quite usual in the years before the First World War. For boys, the custom of breeching persisted, though it was becoming less common. Small infants of either sex wore dresses, and a lad's first pair of trousers (an important milestone in his young life) might well be commemorated in a photograph. There was no universally accepted age for breeching — it could be as early as three and as late as eight. In poorer families the age might simply be that at which a pair of breeches became available by virtue of a boy's immediate senior growing out of them. On average, at any rate, the age probably went down as time progressed. Photographs of a known boy in a dress are likely to date from before the Great War; if he is other than very small, the earlier years of the century are more likely.

Beyond that, there are one or two isolated observations that can be made about children's clothes in the first 40 or so years of the century. Large bows in girls' hair were popular during the First World War and for a year or two on either side of it, and boys often wore open-necked soft shirt collars from the 1930s onwards. But increasingly common for boys, as the century advanced, was the school uniform comprising peaked cap, jacket, short trousers and long socks decorated with bands of colour at the top. The jacket might be a blazer, or it might be made up in grey fabric to match the trousers and turn the ensemble into a suit. Such uniforms are occasionally seen in pictures from the 1920s, when only the more select and image-conscious schools were likely to demand them. They were more widespread in the 1930s, though still far from the norm. By the end of the 1940s they had become quite usual. Boys' short trousers, which were worn knee-length at the start of the century, ended above the knee from the 1920s onwards.

Finally, a word about lack of clothes: photos of naked babies on rugs belong to the 20th rather than the 19th century. The fad was an Edwardian introduction and had no place in the Victorian repertoire.

The generations diverge

After the Second World War there was a fresh blossoming of fashion. For women who could afford it there was 'The New Look', introduced by Christian Dior in 1947. This did away with square and padded shoulders and was characterised by fitted tops, tight waists and full, rather longer skirts. Coats and jackets were often beltless, wide and bell-like, and fairly narrow skirts might be worn with them by way of contrast. Wide-brimmed hats, turned down at the front and sometimes referred to as 'flying saucer hats', also derived from this first Dior collection. But small head-hugging hats — amounting to little more than skullcaps — also enjoyed some popularity. Sleeves were often of three-quarter length; stiletto heeled shoes were in vogue; and there was an emerging taste for polka dots.

Whilst, of course, the majority of women were not spending out on high fashion, its characteristics did find their way in diluted form into more everyday clothing, for there was an increase in mass production and ready-to-wear garments.

During the 1950s, designers were showcasing new lines every year. Towards the end of the decade a straight-up-and-down, tubular 'sack' dress was launched (precursor of the tunic and the mini-dress), and skirts became narrower. In theory, the frequent appearance of new styles makes the dating of costume easier for the expert but harder for the bewildered layperson. In practice, however, most people were not dressing themselves as fashion plates or changing their wardrobe on an annual basis. Life for most people was far removed from the catwalk, and the 1940s' focus on the serviceable had not wholly dissolved.

One manifestation of this everyday reality was knitwear. Woollen jumpers, cardigans, pullovers and even dresses were common — perhaps as a legacy of the wartime emphasis on knitting for victory. In the years of clothes rationing, an ability to knit garments had been very valuable. Now mothers, grandmothers and aunts still had the knitting skills, and they continued to use them, sometimes (as a brighter age beckoned) to more colourful effect than before.

But a new element was insinuating itself into the story of costume. The generations were starting to diverge. As austerity receded, a class of moneyed youth was emerging. Until they married and settled down, these young people had spare cash to dispose of. Since the obvious duty of the enterprising was to help them spend it, markets in clothing and entertainment developed to cater for their needs. The teenager had been born. As a result, a separate set of fashions may be identified in photographs and may help with the business of dating.

In the 1950s young women began to be seen in tight sweaters. Often these had rolled-over polo necks, but their most striking feature was the emphasis they gave to the bosom and to the fact that it was made up of two component parts. Belts were often wide, to draw attention to narrow waists. Trousers became popular for casual wear. They fitted more closely than their workwear forerunners and sometimes, in a variation known as Capri pants, their legs ended some way above the ankle. They were often accompanied by flat, ballet-type shoes or slip-on sandals. Towards the end of the decade wide rock-and-roll skirts came into favour, falling to calf-length and held out by stiff nylon petticoats. While their mothers still permed their hair, framing the face in waves or curls, teenage daughters experimented with other options. They might grow their hair long and catch it up behind in a pony-tail; or they might have it cropped short in imitation of Audrey Hepburn, or shorter (in an urchin cut) in homage to Jean Seberg.

Young men, too, were starting to dress differently from their fathers. The sports jacket, with open neck or tie, provided a look that the generations kept in common, but short-bodied baseball jackets or windcheaters were also becoming established, as were leather jackets for those with motorcycles. The most famous male style of the time, however, was the Teddy boy look. Predominantly a minority fashion and a working class phenomenon, the Teddy boy style (in theory at least) recaptured the finery of the Edwardian era. Long heavy jackets came almost down to the knees. Lapels were long, narrow and — like cuffs and pockets — trimmed with velvet. Ties were thin, and the soles of shoes were thick. Tight-legged 'drainpipe' trousers ended at the ankle, allowing the socks to be seen. Hair was grown long and swept back in luxuriant and well-lubricated waves.

More significant for the majority of young people was the arrival of denim jeans. Already long established in the US, jeans reached the UK in the mid-1950s and young women were not slow to follow young men in adopting them.

Trousers in general, and jeans in particular, were at the heart of a new development. It was becoming possible for certain garments to be worn by both sexes. The duffel coat — heavy, hooded and fastened by a series of loops and barrel-shaped buttons — confirmed the trend. Add the fact that many young women had their hair cut short and it was impossible, their disgruntled elders averred, to tell the sexes apart. So, in John Osborne's *The Entertainer* (first performed in 1957), Billy Rice complained, "Why, half the time you can't tell the women from the men. Not from the back. And even at the front you have to take a good look, sometimes." He may have been exaggerating a little, but he was speaking for a generation.

The sixties and after

Clothes from the 1960s onwards may be of some interest, but the photographs that show them can hardly be described as old. So no systematic account of the rest of the century's clothes is attempted. But, since some of us have been no better than our ancestors at documenting our snaps, a few brief notes are offered by way of an aide mémoire.

1960s: neat, Italian-style clothing (early 60s); simple geometrical patterns; bold colours; tunic-like dresses; mini-skirts, ending well above the knee (1964 on, and growing shorter by the year); trouser suits (second half of decade); PVC, especially for rainwear; pale faces and lipstick; boots as accompaniment to miniskirts (late 60s); men's high-necked jackets, with or without lapels; Beatles haircuts; the disappearance of turn-ups (mid-60s); the beginnings of 'flower power' and psychedelia (1967).

1970s: height of flower power (earlier 70s especially); midi- and maxi-skirts gaining in popularity; shaggy Afghan coats; cheesecloth shirts; ponchos; flared trousers; vigorous, swirling ('psychedelic') patterns;

cloaks; kaftans; hot pants; tie-dyeing; beads, flower motifs and headbands; platform shoes; long hair for both sexes; large, floppy shirt collars; 'punk', with customisation of clothes and bodies (late 1970s).

<u>1980s</u>: 'punk' sufficiently established to be a tourist attraction; power dressing; padded shoulders; skirts above the knee; short, flared ('rah rah') skirts; big hair; Princess Diana hairstyle (after 1981 royal wedding); bagginess (of T-shirts, jackets, trousers, sweaters); tracksuits and legwarmers worn outside the gym; logos; New Romanticism (frilly shirts, lace, trainers, dark lipstick, lined eyes).

<u>1990s</u>: the fleece jacket (from early 1990s); smiley face logo (first seen in late 1980s); visible body piercing and tattoos more frequent; ever-baggier jeans and T-shirts (bearing ever-coarser slogans); 'folksy' revival — knitwear, second-hand clothes, echoes of the 70s (late 1990s).

These brief reminders may give the impression that, for the young at least, a primary function of fashion is to shock. If so, that is probably appropriate. An anecdote from 1966, however, serves to remind us that propriety is probably in the eye of the beholder. In that year, it is reported, a young woman arrived at Ascot's royal enclosure wearing a trouser suit. She was turned away. Trousers were still deemed unseemly for ladies. So, a little later, she returned wearing a revealing mini-dress, which ended high on the thigh, and she was admitted with no trouble at all.

Dating the Image —
Special Family Occasions

Sandwiched between discussions of costume and background — and relating to both — two family album specialities demand attention. Weddings and holidays both tend to be particularly well represented in our collections, so some brief account of their clothes and settings is appropriate here. (Books giving more detailed attention to fashions for beach and altar can be found in the bibliography.)

Wedding costume

When the 20th century opened, the bridal gown had not yet become the norm. A bride wore her best clothes, certainly, but the flowers she carried might be as useful an indicator of her status as a white wedding dress. In Edwardian times, too, many women opted for a Sunday-best version of everyday wear. From around 1908 the tailored suit was a common choice, and (at weddings as elsewhere) the huge and heavily decorated hat was much in evidence on the heads of both brides and their guests. But the custom-designed wedding dress was gaining ground. Its hem brushed the ground and a general softness of effect was helped by the liberal use of lace and chiffon. Waists were baggy and pouched, like the blouses of the time, and sleeves were long or of three-quarter length. It was quite common to use a mixture of different fabrics, and this practice survived into the 1920s. From about 1908 some brides dispensed with the hat and wore instead a headdress incorporating a veil. Bouquets were hefty and trailing and might be carried by bridesmaids and mothers, as well as by the bride herself.

For men of the middle classes and above, the standard costume was a black frock coat with straight hem parallel to the ground, pale waistcoat and striped trousers. But the frock coat was already sharing the limelight with the cut-away morning coat, which sloped away from the bottom button to become longer at the back than the front. Working men wore lounge suits, but a touch of formality was likely to be added by a high and starched shirt collar.

During the First World War brides' hemlines became a little higher, starting around the ankle and rising an inch or two by the time that hostilities finished. This meant that a small stretch of leg could be glimpsed, to reveal that a fashion for pale stockings had developed by the end of the war. High necks enjoyed a period in fashion. But a side-effect of war was that the purpose-made wedding dress lost a little of its hold on the occasion. Big hats were still in evidence, but they were often of straw, were likely to be less profusely trimmed, and were generally less demonstrative than their predecessors.

Uniform was not uncommon for grooms, and the morning coat was now more usual than the frock coat amongst the genteel classes. But otherwise the recipe for male wedding attire continued much as before.

The advent of the 1920s saw wedding gown hemlines dip briefly back to the ankle. But it was not long before most brides were choosing shorter dresses. Hems at about calf-length were popular, and the briefer skirts of routine 1920s wear did not make a full transition to wedding fashion. White stockings were now the norm. The disappearance of the waistline — which affected everyday clothes from around 1925 — was echoed in wedding dresses. But this feature is sometimes a little obscured by the elaborate trimmings of brides' clothes and is easier to spot in the dresses of the bridesmaids. The later years of the decade saw a taste for scalloped hems, and its very end was marked by a fashion for uneven hems, with the front higher than the back. Bouquets were still large. Cloche hats were common for bridesmaids, and if the bride wore a headdress with veil, it was likely to be set across the forehead to create a cloche-like horizontal line across the brow.

The morning suit was now the standard wear for men of elevated social standing, but the middle classes were joining the lower orders in the wearing of lounge suits, which were often accompanied by trilby hats. Spats were in vogue.

The 1930s brought a return to floor-length dresses and level hems, and by the end of the decade the wearing of white wedding gowns was firmly established as the usual practice. A romantic neo-medieval look was often striven for, and satin became popular. There was often a design emphasis on the shoulders and upper arms, though the fall of a copious veil might mean that this emphasis was less visible on brides than on bridesmaids. From about 1937 the heart-shaped 'sweetheart' neckline came into favour, and this continued to be popular well into the 1940s. Headdresses with veils were set on top of the head, across the crown rather than the brow. Hats, as chosen by some brides and many guests, tended to have low crowns and wide brims and were worn tilted to one side.

Men continued to dress much as before, though wearers of morning coats now often set them off with a grey rather than a black top hat, and spats faded from the scene towards the end of the decade.

The first two years of the war saw no great changes in wedding fashions, but clothes rationing was introduced in 1941 and austerity soon began to bite. Where the family structure allowed, dresses from the 1930s could be passed on from older to younger sister. But where a new dress was needed, there often had to be a pooling of coupons, and it became necessary to squeeze the maximum effect out of a very limited amount of fabric. Skirts remained long but, to economise on material, they became narrower. Necklines tended to be fairly high and sleeves to be long and tight. There was still some emphasis on the shoulder, which was frequently padded. A long veil might be worn, if an old one could be borrowed or handed down. If a new one had to be made, it was likely to fall no lower than the shoulders.

But plenty of women gave up the idea of the white wedding. The civilians might settle for a utility suit, with straight skirt and pad-shouldered jacket, whilst those who were in the forces might wear uniform. Amongst grooms, uniforms were as common as morning attire was now rare.

After the Second World War white weddings became more common again, though rationing was still in effect. Some dresses, though still quite narrow skirted, managed to run to a small train. Certain fabrics became coupon free. Amongst these was parachute silk, which was fallen on eagerly by home dressmakers (who were now widespread), but which proved more useful for the petticoats that gave a skirt substance than for the frock itself. Wedding dress hire also began to find a place in the scheme of things.

The tradition of grooms kitted out for their country did not disappear immediately. Since peacetime national service replaced war service, young men continued to find themselves in uniform, and a fair number were married in it. The addition of a buttonhole to the uniform was a post-war irregularity adopted by many.

The expanding fashion market meant that a variety of bridal styles was adopted in the 1950s, and there was less uniformity about the dresses. Common tendencies included the fitted bodice, long sleeves, floor length skirts, and rounded or V-shaped (rather than sweetheart or square) necklines. The middle of the decade saw a vogue for wide collars, which stood up and surrounded the neck like the sides of a boat, or which folded down to form a miniature shawl. A headband, with veil hanging down behind, was a popular form of headdress. The dresses of bridesmaids were often shorter than those of brides, ending around mid-calf.

Uniforms were now less common for men. National service continued, but grooms undergoing it were by now keener to get out of the uniform for a special occasion. They were also more likely to be able to afford smart alternative clothing. There were still some who wore morning dress, which was increasingly likely to be hired for the occasion, but it was the dark lounge suits that predominated.

Settings and conventions for wedding photographs

At the end of the Victorian age, wedding pictures (when taken) were still most likely to be the result of a visit to the studio, and such indoor pictures were still being made — though with decreasing frequency — as late as the 1930s. But the Edwardian era saw the growth of what was to become the mainstream tradition: the open-air wedding photograph. With that came the group picture. Groups were not impossible in the studio, and indoor pictures of weddings from the 1920s and 1930s often include several people. But groups were less manageable in the confined surroundings. In Victorian and Edwardian times they were frequently out of the question in any case. Studio shots of bride and groom were often the result of a visit to the photographer on a day before or after the event, when the full family party might not be available. The studio portrait commemorated the event, but the outdoor picture actually recorded the occasion.

Before the First World War, outdoor groups might be arranged in a garden or before a wall, but pictures taken at the church door did not become common until the 1920s. A variety of levels can help the photographer when arranging group pictures, so seating some subjects and letting others stand beside or behind them was a common ploy in the years before the Great War.

It was still sometimes used in the 1920s and 1930s. Perhaps surprisingly — since the problems of composition did not suddenly disappear — all-standing groups seem to have become more usual from the 1940s onward.

A typical feature of Second World War wedding photographs is the group of uniformed soldiers, sailors, firemen or whatever, who were serving with one or both of the chief performers. In fact, they may be more in evidence than bridesmaids, since bridesmaids needed dresses and were therefore sometimes dispensed with in the interest of economy. An image often recorded at these weddings was the triumphal arch formed by colleagues holding up their rifles, bayonets, hats or truncheons for the happy couple to pass under. It was a practice that occasionally had its less bellicose equivalent — so one might sometimes, for example, find a guard of honour made up of Scouts or Wolf Cubs. It was in the immediately post-war years that one further attendant, the pageboy, made his first significant impression on the wedding scene.

The 1950s saw cake-cutting pictures becoming a part of the standard photographic repertoire. For professionals, it had by then become relatively easy to take indoor pictures in places other than the studio. The overcoming of lighting problems also encouraged the rise in the 1950s and (more particularly) the 1960s of pictures taken inside the church. Until then, technical difficulties had combined with a sense of seemliness to keep photographers waiting at the porch.

Seaside costume

In turning from weddings to holidays we move from the extremes of formality to the extremes of informality — though the desire to look memorable may remain.

In the early years of the century, women bathers wore either a two-piece costume (basically a skirted tunic plus voluminous drawers) or a one-piece costume with an overskirt. The one-piece version fairly quickly lost its skirt and became short legged, short sleeved and tight fitting. The two-piece version — with which rather more women felt at ease — allowed possibilities of trimmings and contrasting materials and was sometimes designed in a style reminiscent of the sailor suit. But even this became skimpier. At the beginning of century drawers were tied below the knee, but by 1919 they came very little lower than the skirt of the tunic. There was a brief fashion for wearing stockings with bathing costume, but that died before the first decade was over. Bathing hats were normal, and a variety of styles was affected. But Edwardian bathing hats, like Edwardian hats generally, tended to be big and puffed out rather than head hugging. They might even have whalebone inside to preserve their shape when wet. The first bare heads on the beach and in the sea were seen just before the start of the First World War. But they were rare, and hats for bathing were to remain the norm for some decades yet.

For men, the one-piece swimming costume, complete with legs and arms, was normal. But by 1910 those legs and arms had become quite short. Striped fabrics were usual at beginning of the new century, as they had been at the end of the old. But plain material became more common in the years just before the war. For boys, trunks with very short legs made an appearance in some places before the war, but such brief garments remained fairly unusual for adults until the 1930s. On the beach or promenade, the popularity of blazers and boaters carried over from Victorian times. Now, however, they were generally worn with pale trousers rather than with the dark ones that were usually preferred in the 1890s. A similar colour shift was evident in boys' sailor suits, which were now more likely to be white than dark blue. Panama hats, softer and lighter than boaters, were becoming popular.

In the early 1920s one- and two-piece swimming costumes were both still possible. By now, however, the two-piece garments were often made up of quite short drawers and a simple shift-like tunic without sleeves. (The sleeves dwindled away first, and then the legs became shorter). By the late 1920s the backs of the one-piece swimsuits were often rather lower than the fronts, and the two-piece costume had virtually disappeared. The age of the suntan was beginning, and there was some tension between the desire to acquire a tan and the accepted notions of modesty. (In the USA, inspectors were employed on some beaches to measure costumes and check that no more thigh was revealed than local regulations permitted.) Hats were still generally worn in the sea, and plain rubber bathing caps were common by end of decade.

Horizontally striped costumes for men were now totally old-fashioned, and the standard one-piece bathing suit was shrinking: necks and backs were lower, legs were reduced to just a couple of inches, and sleeves were disappearing to leave little more than a strap-width over the shoulders. Plain dark colours were usual in the early 1920s, but contrasting top halves in a paler colour became popular in the second half of the decade. Hats at the seaside were no longer obligatory, and bare heads were often in evidence on the prom as well as on the beach.

In the 1930s a tan was desirable, and beachwear was designed to provide spaces where it could be acquired. The backs of women's costumes were often very low, sometimes being cut away almost entirely. Crossover straps might be needed at the back, in order to keep the garment on. Sometimes panels were cut out from the side. Occasionally, by the end of the decade, a two-piece of a more modern kind was seen. This was made up of separate trunks and brassière — though both were ample and covered any potentially controversial landmark, including the navel. The late 1930s saw the first use of elasticated fabric and the beginning of a fashion for bright, ruched costumes (their textured surface achieved with the aid of shirring elastic). In the water, white rubber bathing caps were by now pretty well universal, though on the beach it was becoming possible for women to appear bareheaded.

Very short-legged trunks were replacing bathing costumes for younger men in the 1930s. Indeed, it was hard to discern any leg to speak of, except insofar as the garment ended in a horizontal line, parallel to ground, rather than sloping up towards the hip. But men of a more staid disposition continued with the one-piece costume. Shirtsleeves were now acceptable on the prom and the pier as well as on the beach. Boaters had disappeared and panamas were for older men. But jokey sailor hats were now a possibility for those determined to show they were having a good time. Sunglasses began to make their appearance for both men and women, though at this stage they were far more likely to be seen in the USA than the UK.

The Second World War was not a vintage period for family holidays or fun on the beach.

After the Second World War, and on into the 1950s, more elasticised fabrics were used and bright shirred costumes became increasingly common for women. They were ever more cut away at the back and were supported by thinner cross-straps or by ribbons that came from the centre front and tied behind the neck. Sometimes, in the 1950s, costumes had no shoulder straps or halters at all. Their leg-holes sloped up towards the hips instead of being cut straight across in a line parallel to the ground. White rubber bathing caps remained pretty well universal through the 1940s and into the 1950s, at which point some women started to dispense with swimming hats altogether.

The brassière with short skirt was sometimes seen in the 1940s, but the bikini (first seen in US in 1946) didn't reach these shores until the 1950s. This revealing two-piece ensemble was named after the Bikini atoll in the South Pacific, which was used by the US as a nuclear test site. (The notion was, presumably, that such skimpy garb had a similarly explosive impact.)

Trunks rather than costumes were now normal for men of any age group, and they were becoming less substantial, sloping upwards at the hip and leaving the navel uncovered. Elasticated fabrics were starting to replace wool. Sunglasses for both sexes were now spreading to the UK, and they became more common in the 50s, though the fashion-resistant still thought them an affectation.

Seaside settings and conventions

Studios in coastal towns had been catering for the holiday trade with seaside props and backcloths since the 1880s, and some of these settings continued in use during the early 1900s. (A littoral or mast-top background is not, however, a guarantee of a coastal location, since photographs from inland studios with seaside sets turn up from time to time.) What the 20th century added to the professional repertoire was the novelty setting. From its earliest years use was made of mock-up railway carriages and comic picture boards with cut-out apertures through which the customer could peer and so supply the missing features.

But open-air seaside pictures were increasingly common: people were now taking their own cameras out with them, and the professionals too were venturing onto promenade or beach in search of custom. Clues for dating can be sometimes found in the resulting outdoor backgrounds, but they tend to be of a fairly imprecise nature.

Beach vendors of comestibles or novelties are, broadly speaking, likely to date from before the First World War. After the war, the general direction of movement was off the sand and onto the promenade for such retail outlets as stalls, kiosks and tricycle carts. (The Walls ice cream tricycle, with its 'Stop me and buy one' slogan, was first seen in 1922, when it made its début in the London area. During the 1930s it was common both inland and at the seaside.)

Bathing machines generally disappeared between 1900 and 1914, but they survived for different lengths of time in different resorts. They tended to be replaced by bathing tents or beach huts. The tents were still in evidence in some places in the late 1920s and even into the 1930s.

It can be worth looking out for signs of civic investment in the area close to the sea. Between the wars most seaside towns spent heavily on their seafronts. Blackpool, for instance, spent £1½ million. Events and attractions — such as carnivals, parades, entertainments and floral displays — were then devised to make use of the space that had been provided. So evidence of a developed promenade (rather than just an uncluttered walking space) suggests the 1920s or later.

As a result of this kind of development, strolling along the seafront became, in itself, part of the holiday experience, and photographers were at hand to record it. So at the sea as elsewhere, the 1920s and (even more particularly) the 1930s gave rise to pictures of people walking along. Photographers haunted the prom, snatching shots of passers-by in the hope of turning the occasion into a sale. The promenade photographer was also active in the years after the Second World War, though in gradually decreasing numbers. By the 1960s some were driven to such dubious gimmicks as offering poses with tame animals and birds, as they attempted the increasingly difficult task of enticing customers.

Sometimes a background of live-in chalets or organised entertainments and activities may suggest that a picture was taken at a holiday camp. Holiday camps were a phenomenon that blossomed in 1930s: Billy Butlin opened his first establishment at Skegness in 1936, others followed suit, and there were 200 camps in Britain by the outbreak of war. For a few years after the war, until late 1940s, the holiday camp still enjoyed some middle class patronage. It was, perhaps, a brief post-war period of inter-class solidarity. After that, camp patrons were generally working class. This means that a holiday camp picture of middle-class family members is unlikely to date from the 1950s or later.

Defences against possible invasion were set up during the war, especially along the Channel coast. Any picture showing scaffolding or wire on a beach is, therefore, likely to indicate 1939 or later. The war, as already observed, was not a peak time for the seaside holiday. But, when it was over, the defences were not all cleared away very quickly. People nevertheless returned to the seaside. So beach pictures showing both defences and people are likely to indicate the second half of the 1940s, when the war had ended but the structures had not yet been dismantled.

Dating the Image — Backgrounds

Indoor backgrounds

The convenient succession of fashions that characterised the Victorian studio had no clear counterpart in the workplace of the 20th century professional. Distinctive new traditions of backcloth did not develop, except in the case of the seaside novelty settings. The 1890s fashion for vignetted close-ups, at least for individual portraits, had perhaps rather stunted the development of the traditional pictorial backdrop. In the 20th century, therefore, studio backgrounds were often neutral. Some were wholly plain and some were textured, but in neither case was a sense of specific location conveyed.

Pictorial settings did not, however, disappear completely overnight. Many studios were still furnished with backdrops from earlier years, and if these hadn't become too creased by rolling and unrolling, they could still be called into service in the period before and during the First World War. The pictorial backgrounds visible in portraits from these years often, therefore, echo the styles prevalent in the 1880s and (where not hidden by vignetting) the 1890s. So we still see some romantic scenes with sylvan glades, distant ruined castles and slightly impressionistic foliage. Also to be found are backcloths of impressive interiors, depicting extensive panelling or a grand staircase down which the subject has supposedly just made a dramatic entrance. But when new backcloths were painted, they don't seem to have created the impetus needed for a convincing new direction in fashion. Occasional examples of contemporary painted scenery are encountered in pictures dating from the 1920s and 1930s. Those not falling into the novelty category may show cottage garden scenes of a kind that was to become popular for chocolate box lids and jigsaws. They may also be rather crudely executed. Studios were declining in numbers, and the scene painting tradition, with its associated skills, had largely disappeared. So it was the neutral background that quickly became (and remained) more characteristic of the 20th century.

Some design aspects of studio furniture and furnishing may afford clues, if the camera is far enough from the subject to allow them to be seen. Whilst the art nouveau style — with the curvilinear leaves and tendrils of its swirling vegetable forms – originated in the 1890s, its influence was still strong in the Edwardian years. The rather more solid yet streamlined geometry of art deco also demonstrated some staying power, still flourishing in the 1930s (the decade after its birth). Sometimes the back of a studio chair or the shape of a mirror will show the influence of one or other style and suggest approximate dating possibilities.

But most of the century's photographs were taken outside the studio. Whilst home backgrounds would seem to offer a rather more promising source of evidence for dating, for some decades such backgrounds amounted merely to front door and porch. The family on the doorstep was an immensely popular subject in the early years of roll film, but the camera was unable to go beyond the front door and into realms that were insufficiently lit for photographs. When domestic interiors are found, they have usually been taken by amateurs and must therefore date from the age of flash photography. For most families this period began not with the 1929 arrival of flash, but with the years of its popularity in the 1950s or 1960s.

Outdoor backgrounds

In outdoor photographs there is, at least in theory, some chance of dating the scene from its details. In practice, helpful details may prove elusive. In countryside scenes, for example, there is precious little to date. Flora and fauna can become extinct or be introduced, but they are not in the habit of presenting themselves for inspection in family photographs. Back gardens (tamed bits of countryside) may sometimes be more informative. When two or more pictures of different dates are compared, a study of the growth of background shrubs and trees may suggest the order in which the pictures were taken. Generally, however, identifiable flowers and the degree of leaf cover are more likely to suggest time of year than time of century. (Indeed, in cases of a known location, the direction of shadows may even help you to hazard a guess at time of day.)

In townscapes, buildings are of little help, unless they are both identifiable and either obviously new or just being built. The perfect example of this kind of evidence actually comes from the 19th rather than the 20th century, and from photographs taken by Clementina, Lady Hawarden. It is known that she took up photography in the second half of the 1850s and died in 1864, and that dates her pictures reasonably closely. Consideration of the apparent ages of various daughters, her frequent subjects, can offer further assistance. But Virginia Dodier has been able to suggest even more precise dating for some examples by examining the advance to completion of buildings seen in the hazy background of the Hawardens' South Kensington home.

In streetscapes, the arrival on the scene of certain inventions might be thought to offer an earliest possible date. Unfortunately, however, most such introductions saw the light of day before the 20th century and its outdoor snaps. So the very fact that the picture was taken in the open air may suggest a later date than the earliest possible year indicated by the invention itself. When the 20th century opened, trains were long established, telephones (and, hence, telegraph poles) had arrived, and street lighting was already starting on the transition from gas to electricity. Pneumatic-tyred bicycles with a fairly modern look had been around since the 1880s, and electric trams had started to appear on the streets in the 1890s — when the motorcar had also made its début, with the Prince of Wales taking his first ride in 1898. Whilst the real growth in car numbers did not come until the ten years preceding the First World War, the presence of a car in a picture is no guarantee of a 20th century date. Even manned flight had already made a modest beginning, with Sir Hiram Maxim's Flying Machine travelling through the air for a distance of some three hundred feet in 1894. Admittedly, it was not until the 1900s that the motor-powered bus started to spread. Generally, however, the inventions that the unpractised eye might readily identify were made in the 19th century. They were older than the kinds of photograph most likely to record them, and they are therefore not very useful in dating.

Naturally, expertise could help further. A researcher able to recognise specific models of car, a student familiar with the evolution of street lighting and furniture, or a devotee of early twentieth century public transport could all achieve some success in dating outdoor pictures. Unlike some of the works mentioned in the bibliography, this book can pretend to no such kinds of skill. But it can scatter a few crumbs of potentially relevant information.

Particular buildings and landmarks may sometimes provide an earliest or latest possible date. The Selfridge's shop in London was opened in 1909, for example, Newcastle's New Tyne Bridge was completed in 1928, and the

Crystal Palace at Sydenham burnt down in 1936. The chance of mentioning here a landmark that helps with any one reader's dating problem is, of course, minimal. But where the possibility of that kind of clue is suspected, local research may be worth undertaking. This is particularly true when shops appear in the background. If the area is known, shop signs can be checked against trade directories, which offer a useful record of a street's changing population of traders and other businesses.

Street lighting offers no easy answers to the inexpert eye. Electric luminaires first began to appear in London as early as 1878, but streets lit by gas were still fairly familiar in the 1940s, and isolated pockets of gas lighting could still be found for many years after that. Once again, where the kind of lighting can be identified, local research could lead to a latest or earliest possible date for a scene.

Street features relating to traffic can prove more helpful. White lines were first painted down the middle of roads in 1925, and traffic lights spread after their 1926 introduction in London's Piccadilly. The mid-30s saw the introduction of illuminated orange globes set on black-and-white striped poles to mark pedestrian crossings. (They were named Belisha beacons after the 1934 Minister of Transport.)

Vehicles

As road traffic grew, vehicles of one kind or another were increasingly likely to form part of a street background. The T Model Ford started life in the United States, where it was introduced in 1908. By the mid-20s it was facing serious competition in the UK from the Morris Cowley and the Morris Oxford. But it was not until after the Second World War (and, more particularly, in the 1950s) that car ownership in Britain started to become widespread. The Citroen 2CV, launched in France in 1949, and the Volkswagen 'Beetle', first produced in Germany in 1936, became familiar on our roads during the 1950s. Estate cars, with a wooden trim that gave a characteristically half-timbered look, also became part of the scene from the middle of the decade. The Mini was first seen in 1959.

As a very rough guide, until the 1940s cars tended to have a fairly angular appearance. Those introduced (or redesigned) in the 1950s often had a rather bulbous, round-nosed appearance. Certainly this was true of such popular models as the Morris Oxford and Minor 1000, the Vauxhall Vanguard and the Hillman Minx.

The history of car registration plates dates back to 1883, but the structure of the codes has changed over the years. They can, therefore, sometimes provide an earliest possible date. Until 1904 the recipe was simply: letter, number, letter. Then more complicated codes were brought in. From 1904 until 1932 new number plates showed one or two letters followed by up to four figures. In 1932 the formula was changed to three letters preceding up to three figures. This lasted until 1953, when new registrations continued with the same components but put the figures first. 1963 brought the first use of a suffix letter to denote the year, and this became mandatory in 1965. Thus the pattern became: three letters, up to three numerals, suffix letter. This brings us well into what might reasonably be considered modern times. But, for the record, when an alphabet of suffixes had been completed, 1983 saw a new sequence: prefix letter, up to three figures, and three letters.

L-plates were introduced in 1934, when passing a driving test became a requirement for new motorists.

There are a handful of points that can be made about buses without having to go into the problems of identifying specific models. Motorbuses became common during the early years of the century, making their first appearance in London in 1910. At first they were open-topped. Roofed buses were not seen on the London streets until 1925. Even then the open-topped variety did not disappear immediately from mainstream use, and it enjoyed a revival — for its novelty value — in some seaside towns after the Second World War. Trolley buses were added to the public transport scene in some areas from the mid-30s. They began to die out in the 1950s.

Electric trams may prove more helpful. They can contribute towards dating without even having to appear in the picture. Rails set into the road and wires overhead are as much an indication of their use as an actual vehicle. (Wires alone are not enough for a diagnosis, since overhead wires without rails are an indication of trolley buses rather than trams.) Trams came into service and were abandoned at different times in different towns: the earliest ones appeared in the Victorian age, but the first discontinuation of an electric system came in 1917, at Sheerness. Thereafter, the story of tramways is one of successive abandonments. Eventually, the Great Orme found itself home to Wales' only remaining service in 1960; the closure of the Grimsby and Immingham line left Blackpool as England's only survivor in 1961; and Scotland's last tramway closed in Glasgow in 1962. If the locality of a picture with evidence of trams is known, *The Directory of British Tramways*, by Keith Turner, holds information about every passenger service system that was introduced.

Cycling was another popular way of getting around. In the years from 1900 to the First World War the bicycle had already taken on, in essence, the look of the modern machine. Saddles were sprung, handlebars and wheel rims were nickel-plated, and bells, mudguards, carriers, pumps, lamps, gears and dynamos all made an appearance during this period. But, nickel-plating aside, the cycles were uniformly dark and generally conveyed an impression of something solid and basic. Lighter machines started to appear during the second half of the 1920s, and hub dynamos (possible but relatively uncommon in earlier years) came into widespread use in the 1930s. Evidence of complicated gear systems is also likely to point to the 1930s or later. In the 1940s and more especially the 1950s, fancier finishes and brighter colours were often used. Whilst the actual colours will not be apparent in black and white photos, it may well be evident that a lighter shade than black has been used, that some contrast of tone has been introduced, or that decorative bands or chevrons have been applied. Some bicycles with noticeably smaller wheels found favour in the 1960s. (The first of these, the Moulton Urban Bicycle, came on the market in 1962.)

Some pictures of cyclists seem to have a strong social dimension, and they are likely to belong to the decade before the Second World War. The relatively cheap machines of the 1920s had made cycling a very easily afforded pastime, and the following decade marked the golden age of cycle tours and outings. The rise of the private car in the post-war years made roads less agreeable places. So there is a very good chance that pictures showing leisure cycling (as opposed to do-it-yourself town transport) date from the 1930s or a few years before. Tandems, though not newly invented, enjoyed a burst of popularity during these years, cycling clubs flourished, and it became acceptable for women to pedal in shorts.

Special events

Special events bring out the photographer in us all. Queen Victoria's Diamond Jubilee in 1897 produced a land full of decorations, processions and celebrations asking to be recorded. But though the occasion coincided with the very early years of roll film, the massive boom in its use was still to come. It was the 20th century that saw the growth.

Where a picture shows what seems to be a major public celebration, there are a number of obvious possibilities to check out. Could it depict a coronation? (The century saw four.) Could it commemorate the relief of Mafeking in 1901, or the end of the Great War? (It should, incidentally, be noted that the nationwide peace celebrations were held in June 1919 and marked the Treaty of Versailles rather than the previous November's Armistice Day.) But one-off occasions were not the only pretexts for decorations and junketing. May Day festivities, Empire Day processions and any number of local pretexts for public show should also be considered.

If a special event seems to be the subject of a picture, and if the locality is known, it may be possible to obtain useful advice on the nature and date of the occasion from archivists, libraries, local history societies or newspaper records. Celebrations of an annual kind may present problems. Major mishaps and disasters were happily less regular in their occurrence and may therefore be more easily identified.

A case history illustrates the point well. A collection of roll-film negatives, bought at a King's Lynn market, included several photographs of a flooded town. When printed, the pictures turned out to include a horse and cart splashing past shoe and pie shops, and a boy paddling along with his boots hung by the laces around his neck. Above the boy, on the wall of a building behind him, was a road name, 'Cowgate Street'. Given the Norfolk origin of the find, it seemed reasonable to start by considering Norfolk towns, and particularly towns large enough to have been walled in the past. Since King's Lynn itself had several gates but no Cowgate, the next obvious contender was Norwich. A look at a modern map was enough to establish that the city still has a street called Cowgate. After that, it simply took a trip to the record office, where expert help quickly produced the information that Norwich had been flooded in 1912. The Cowgate area had been affected, and the archivist was able to add that Reeves' Pie Shop, past which the horse was wading in the other picture, had been in nearby Magdalen Street.

But though this story is a pleasant example of success, it has to be admitted that dating special event photographs from their background may often have more to do with serendipity than with system.

Dating Your Own Photographs

There sometimes comes a day when, to our embarrassment, the photographs we need to date are our own. Our ancestors, we realise, were not unique in their ability to leave pictures undocumented, and we really ought to get something done about the drawer full of images from our own earlier years.

Some incidental help towards dating such photos may already have been given when such topics as instamatics and costume were touched on. With relatively recent images, however, the family's own memory of itself will prove the best source of assistance. Inevitably, certain events will provide landmarks. ("She's wearing a ring, so it must be after she married," or, "It looks as if Philomel is still in nappies," or "That's Uncle Alf, and he died in 1982.") In such cases, we are simply using the traditional evidence of births, marriages and deaths in a slightly different way. But less momentous events can also help jog the memory, and we often remember one occurrence in relation to another. ("I changed to contact lenses in the year we went to Venice," or "You still had your moustache when you went to work at Gradgrind's".) If problems of dating persist, it may therefore be worth taking a systematic approach to such milestones and drawing up a family chronology chart.

Start with a well-spaced list of years, allowing plenty of space for adding events. (Creating such a chart on a computer will, of course, avoid the problems that arise when you find you haven't left enough room for a particularly eventful year.) Births, marriages and deaths provide the obvious starting point. Once those have been filled in, the details to be entered will vary from family to family. Moves to a new home are likely to appear, as are changes of school and, perhaps, changes of job. Comings of age and key wedding anniversaries might be appropriate. Changes of car may have to be recalled, whether or not vehicles appear in pictures. (Somebody may recall the difficulty she had getting in and out of a particular car when wearing the dress in the photo.) Holidays may need to be listed and ordered. There may, too, be details relating to specific individuals and their permanent or long-term changes in hair length, facial hair, spectacle wearing, ear piercing and the like. Anything is worth considering that could prompt somebody's memory or that could provide an earliest or latest possible date.

Such a chronology is best worked on, for a while at least, in committee. What one member of the family recalls may spark off a contribution from another. Talking to relatives is as useful in this area of family research as in any other. There is, though, one possible difference. It is standard advice that the family historian should consult elderly relatives. When it comes to fairly recent photographs, it is worth consulting the younger members of the family, too. What parents have forgotten, their children may have no difficulty in remembering.

Illustrations and Dating Charts

The pictures and charts that follow form a kind of reference section.

To allow comparisons to be made easily, the illustrations are grouped together by theme, rather than distributed throughout the text. Figures 1-8 are examples of different formats and processes; figures 9-28 illustrate developments in fashion during the first half of the century; figures 29-32 are devoted to weddings; figures 33-36 focus on the seaside holiday.

It should be borne in mind that dates on the charts can often be only approximate. Whilst some of the details they include are applicable to quite a long time span, the combined evidence of two or three details can often narrow the dating possibilities considerably.

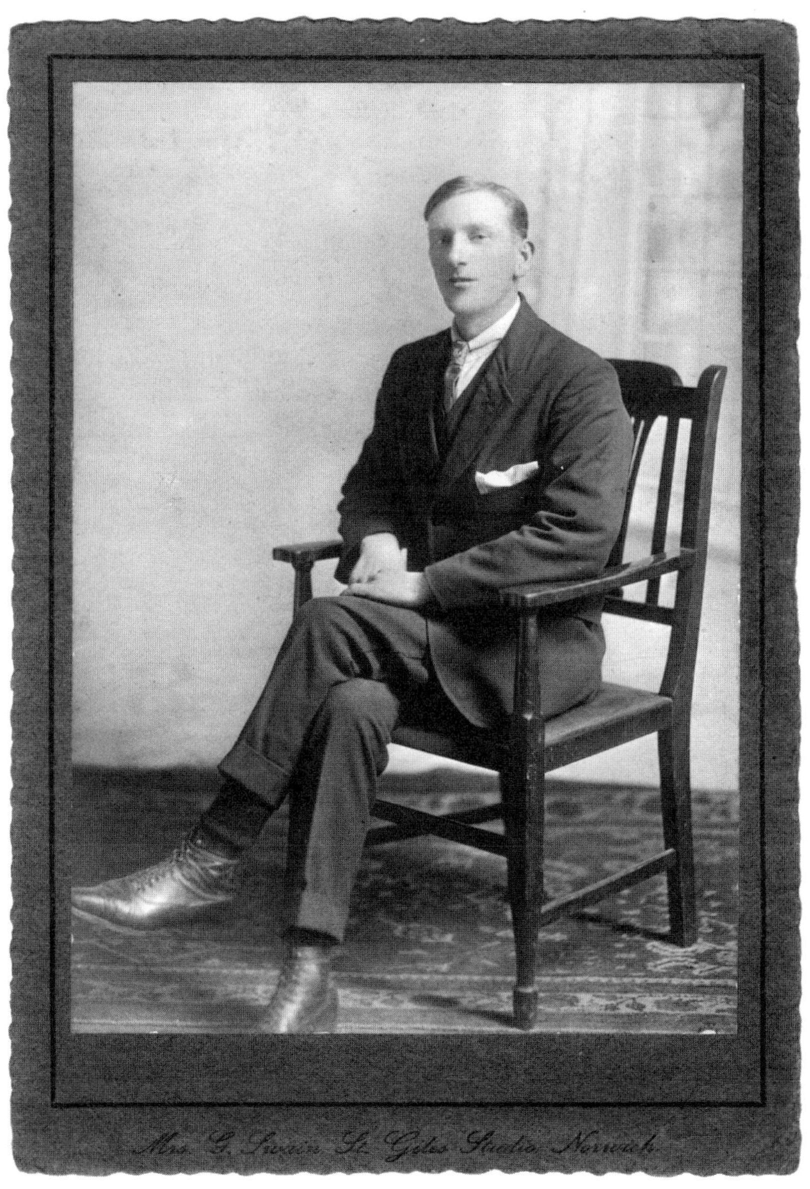

Figure 1: Cabinet print; Mrs G Swain, Norwich. Though introduced earlier, turn-ups were common from about 1912; but directory evidence suggests this picture could date from as late as 1916.

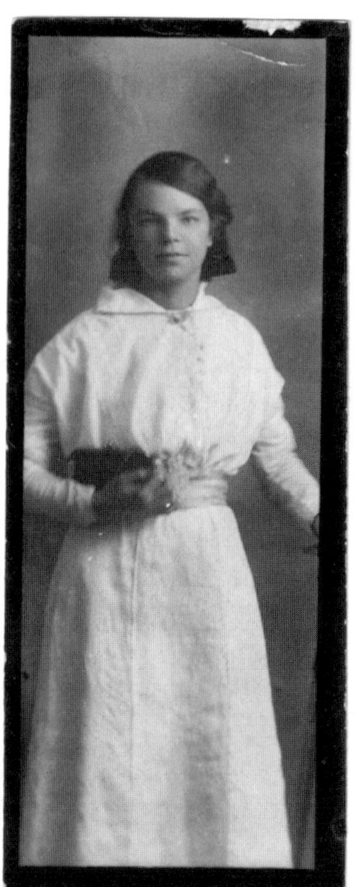

Figure 2: Coupon print; Alan Rufford, Nottingham. Miss B Tandy's likeness appears in one of the Edwardian novelty formats introduced when cartes and cabinet prints lost their hold on the market.

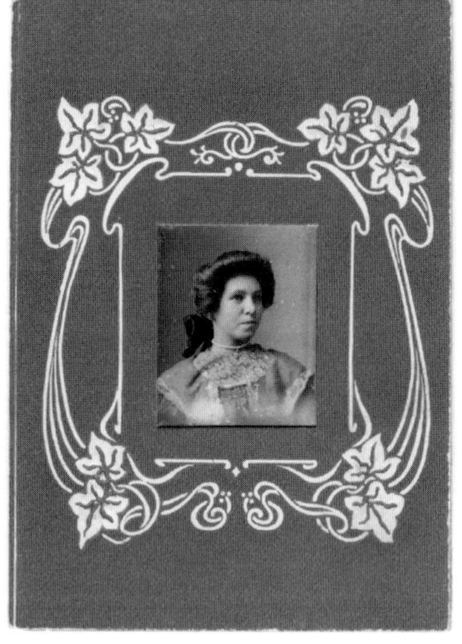

Figure 3: 1 x 1¼ inch print, mounted to approximate carte de visite size. Whilst the design trend straddled the centuries, the muted green card and the woman's hairstyle suggest the latter part of the Art Nouveau period.

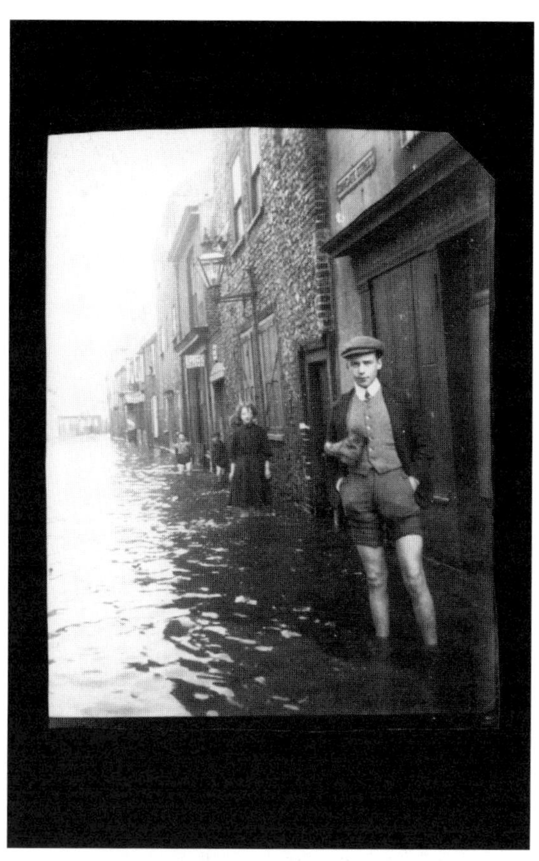

Figure 4: Modern contact print from a 4¼ x 3¼ inch roll-film negative. Since the negative is relatively large, a folding camera rather than a box camera may have been used for this picture of the 1912 Norwich floods.

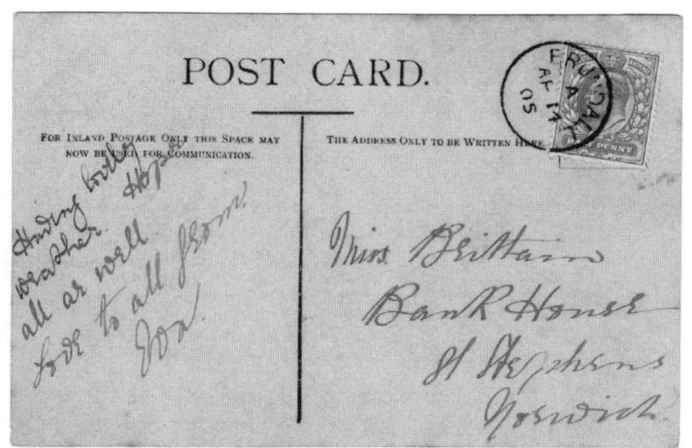

Figure 5: Postcard. Were the 1905 postmark not clearly visible, dating could still be attempted. 'May now be used' would suggest 1902-6, and the yellowish-green stamp would indicate November 1904 or later.

97

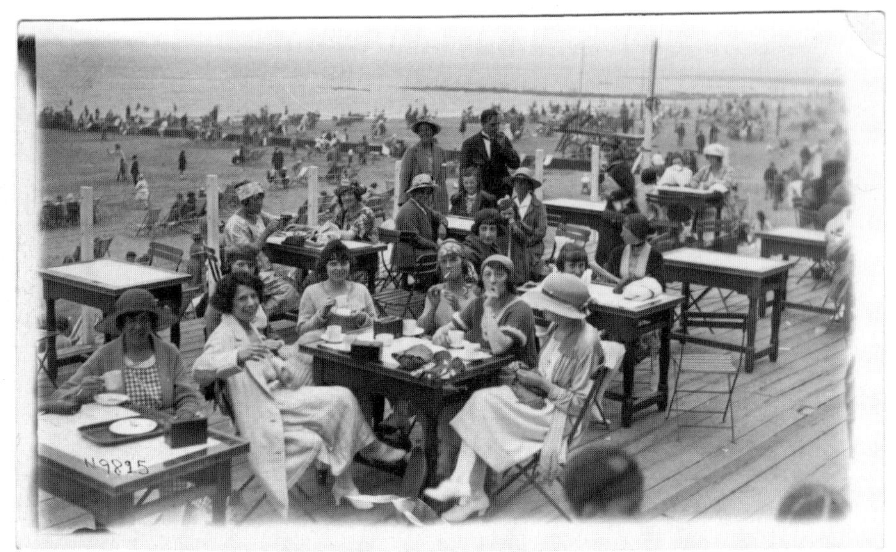

Figure 6: Postcard. The format remained long in favour. The headgear places this scene in the 1920s (when women had started to smoke in public).

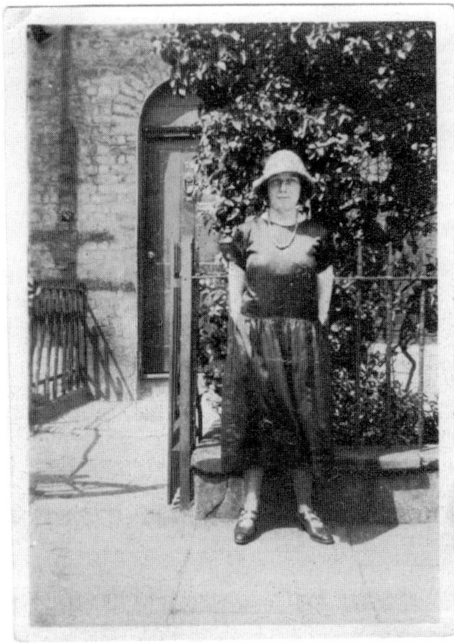

Figure 7: Roll-film print. The picture size is that given by generations of Box Brownies. The word 'Velox' on the back shows that this 1920s example has been printed on chloride developing out paper.

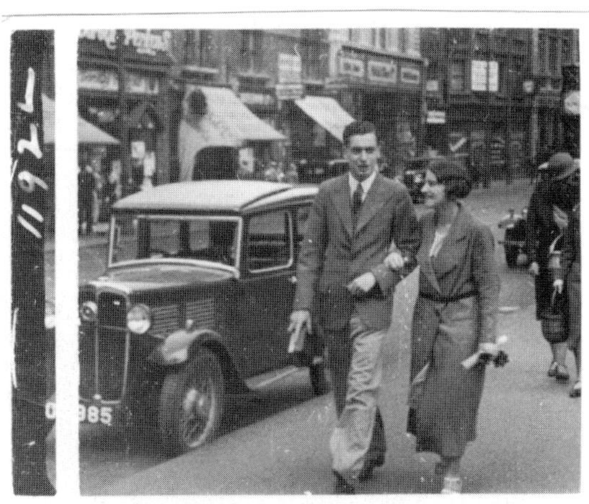

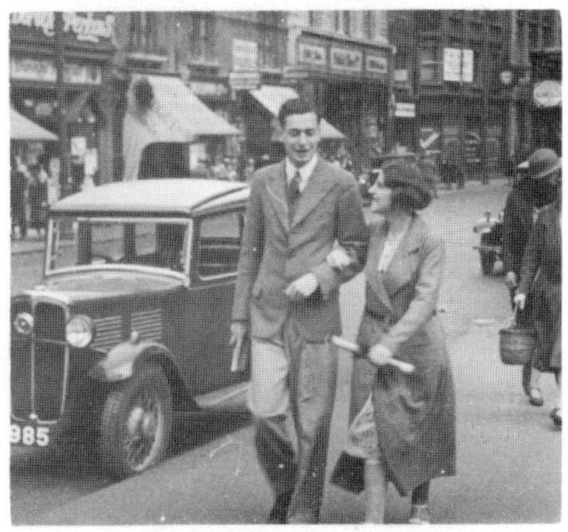

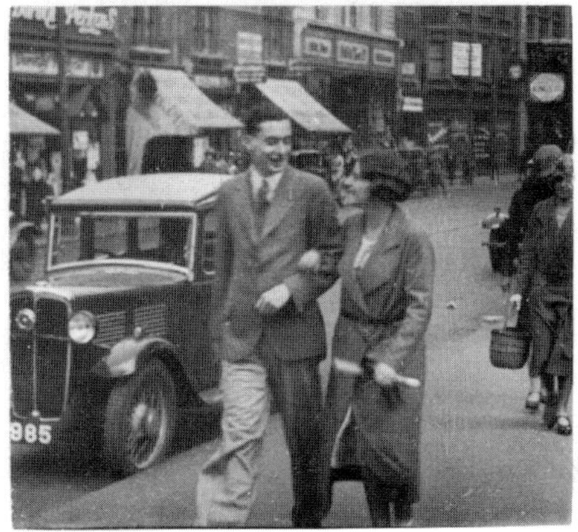

Figure 8: Print strip. The unknown street photographer has opted for novelty rather than the more usual postcard format. The car was registered no later than 1933, and the handwritten date on the back is August 1932.

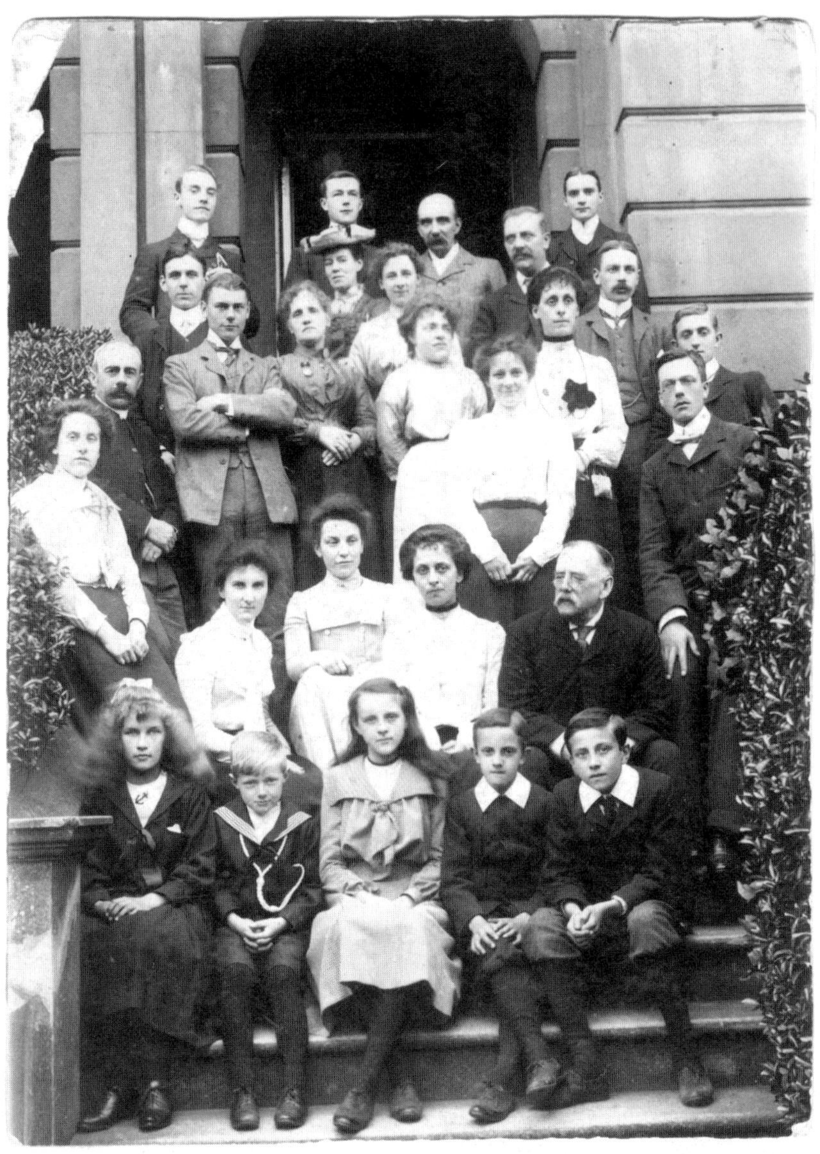

Figure 9: Print mounted to cabinet card size. Pencilled on the back: '1900 approx. Hastings'. Men's high collars, women's blouses and skirts, one forward-looking hat and one old-fashioned dress combine to support the suggestion.

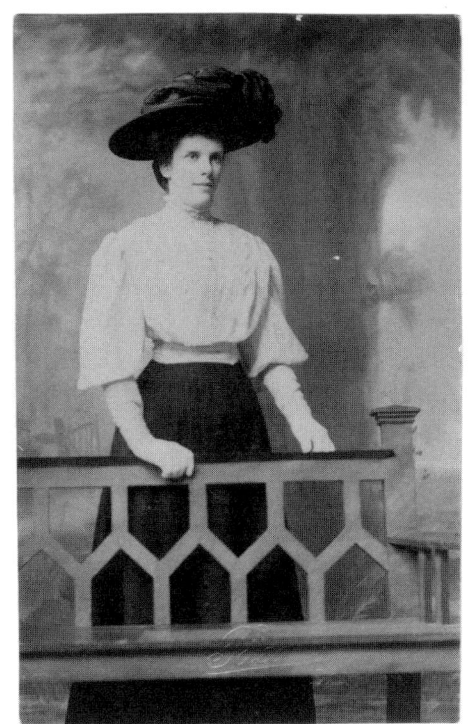

Figure 10: Postcard. The blouse (with rather baggy front and tight cuffs) and the broad hat suggest the second half of the century's first decade. Should the backcloth be considered impressionistic, or merely half-hearted?

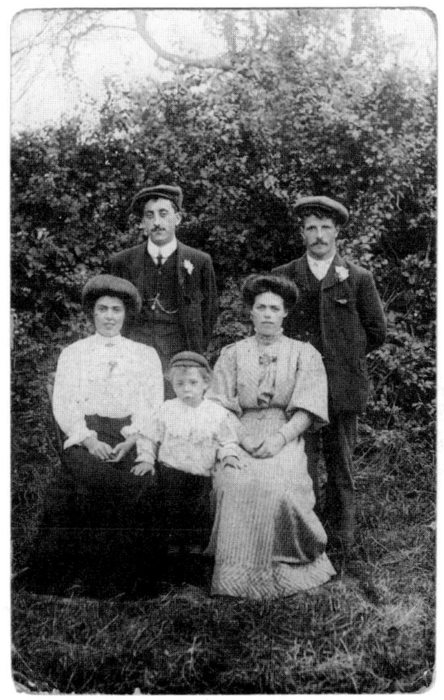

Figure 11: Postcard. The women's long and full skirts, high collars and big hair are characteristically Edwardian. The working class impression of the cloth caps is borne out by below-stairs gossip on the back.

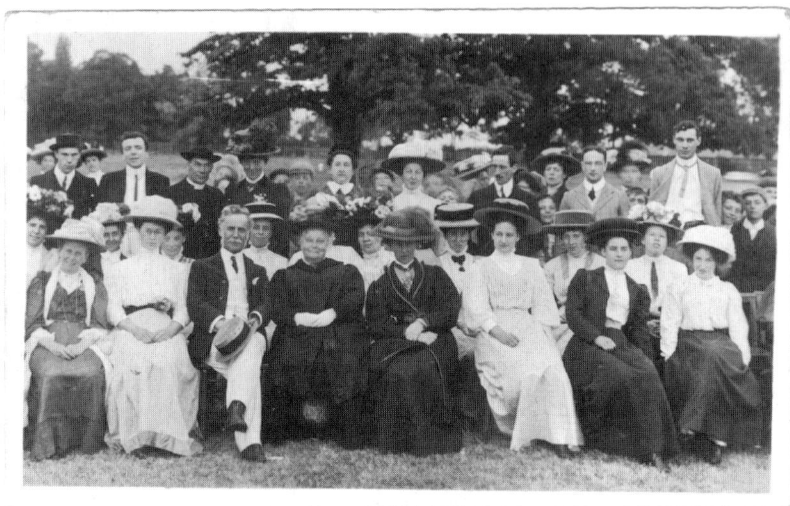

Figure 12: Postcard. The back is postmarked 'Au 14 09'. By now the age of the gateau-style hat is in full swing, but not all blouses have completely lost their bagginess. Pale dresses have a summery feel.

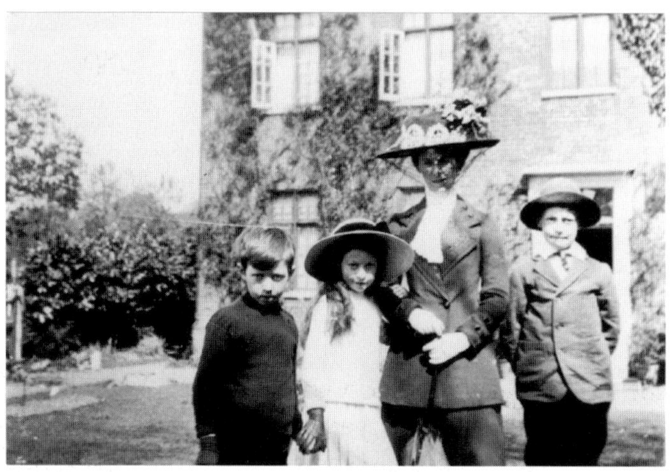

Figure 13: Modern enlargement from roll film negative. Early Georgian hat, lace and tailored suit compete with gurning child for attention. The bedrooms (in accordance with Mrs Beeton's precepts) are being given a healthy airing.

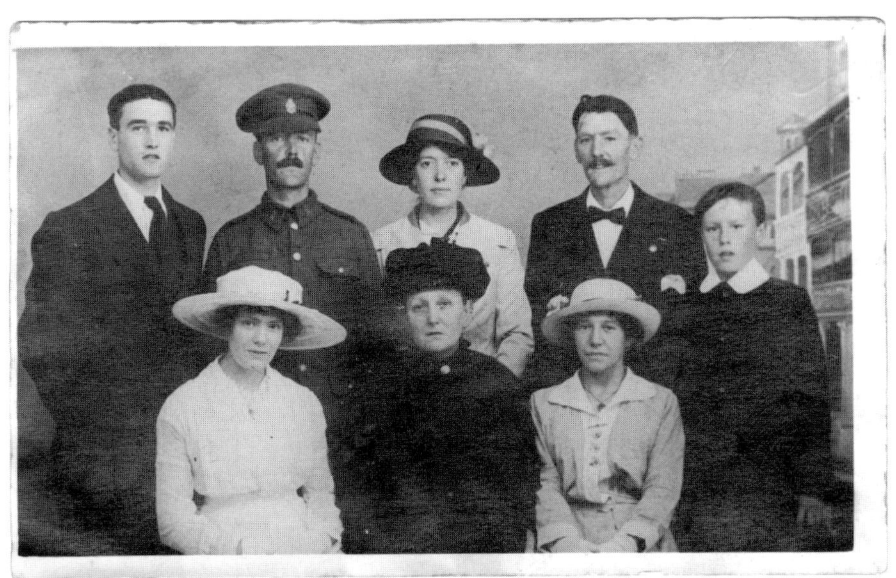

Figure 14: Postcard. The V-neck had appeared just before the First World War, during which pictures of men in uniform regularly marked partings and reunions. Apprehension, rather than relief, seems to prevail on this occasion.

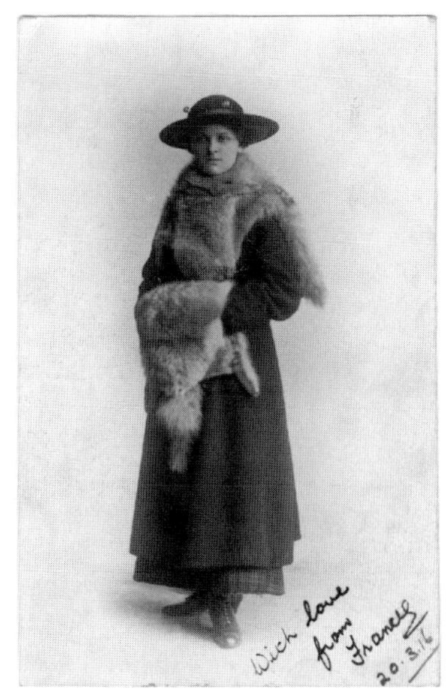

Figure 15: Postcard. Broad-brimmed hats survived into the war years, but unadorned and rounded crowns were already prefiguring the cloche. Boots were commonly worn and skirt lengths allowed them to be seen. But furs were not yet a majority taste.

103

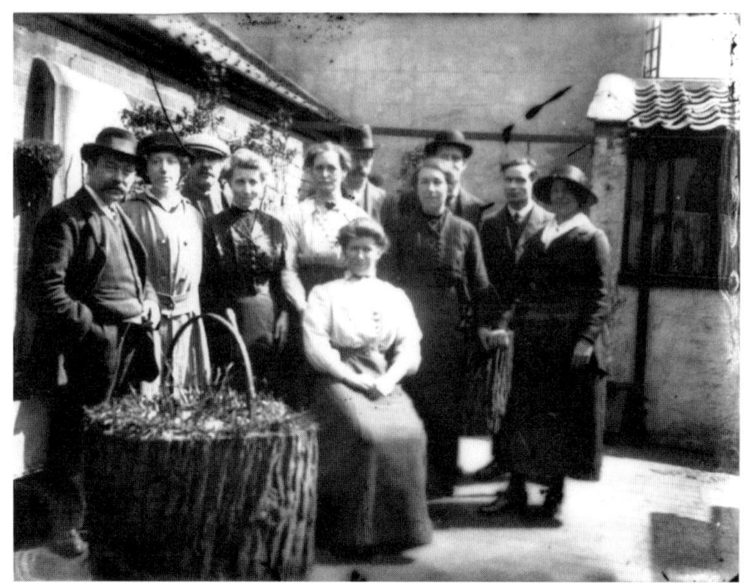

Figure 16: Modern contact print from a half-plate glass negative. The practical clothes of the woman on the right suggest the First World War, and her hem-length indicates its latter days. The variety of men's hats is characteristic of the age.

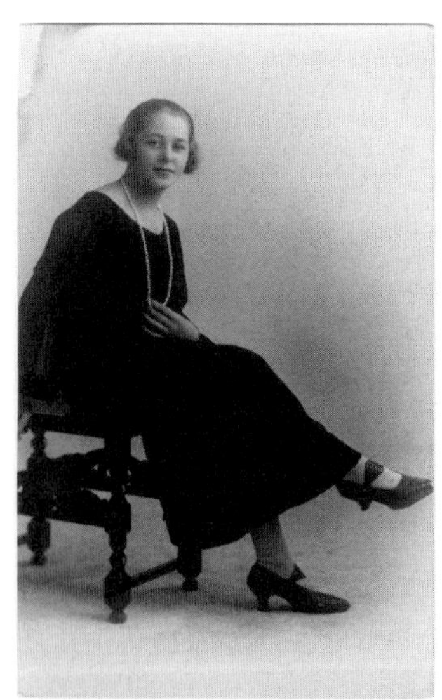

Figure 17: Postcard; Fred Ash, Blackpool and Liverpool. Strappy shoes, beads and sideways pose are all characteristic of their era in this photograph from 1924. Notice, too, the diaphanous fabric of the sleeves.

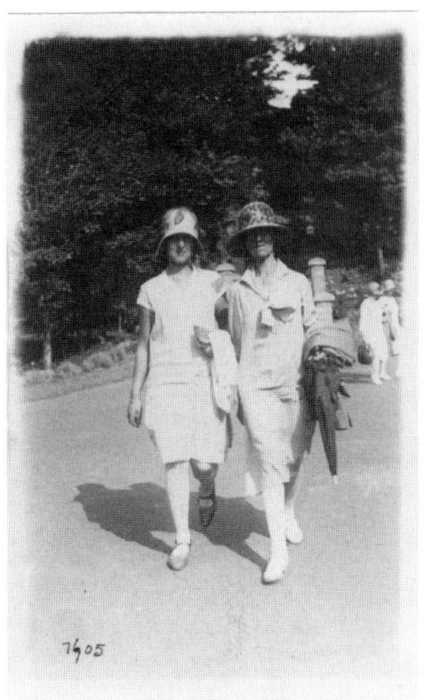

Figure 18: Postcard. Cloche hats and lost waistlines mark this as a picture from the 1920s, and the knee-length hemline didn't appear until about the middle of the decade. The age of the 'striding out' photo has begun.

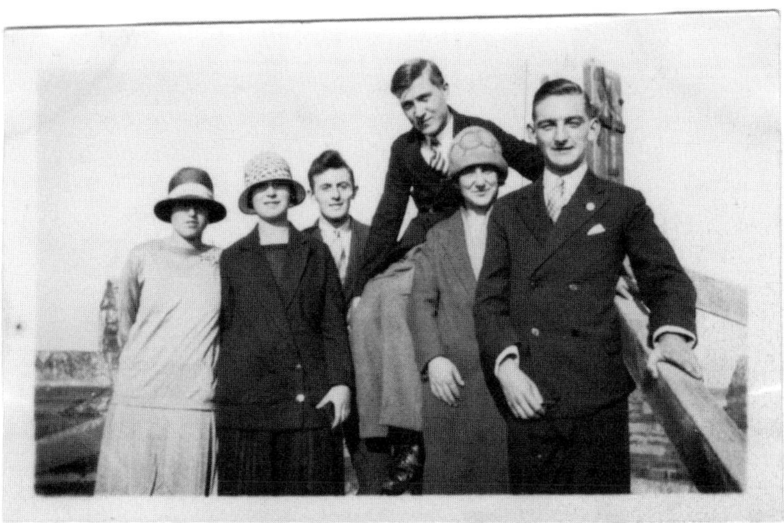

Figure 19: Roll film print, 2½ x 1⅝ inches. Perhaps taken by one of the last Kodak Vest Pocket cameras. There are cloche hats and low waistlines for women, and baggy trousers and double-breasted jackets for men. 'Sept 1928' is written on the back.

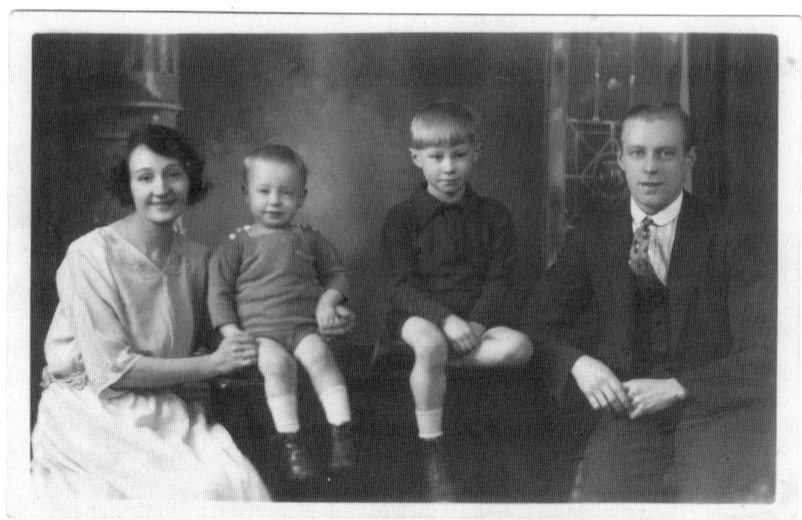

Figure 20: Postcard. Dated 17th January 1926. The mother's simple, collarless dress emphasises her neck in a way that is typical of the age, and there is a bright assertiveness about the father's tie. Pictorial studio backcloths were not quite extinct.

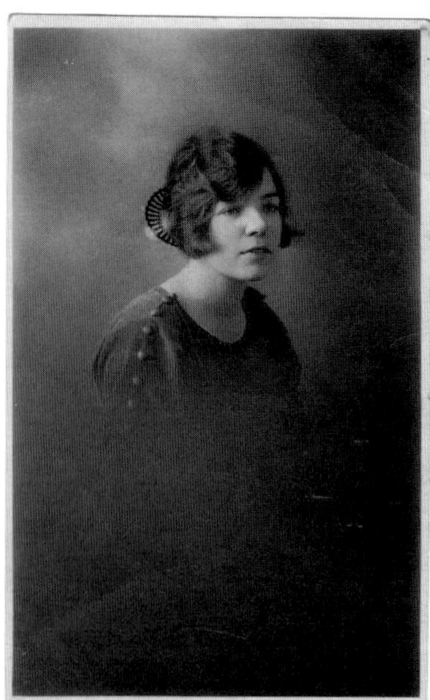

Figure 21: Postcard; James H Jamieson, Preston, Wrexham, Nelson and Walsall. The neckline and hair are of the 1920s, but the decorative comb heralds the 1930s. Body angle and lighting are influenced by fashion and cinematic photography.

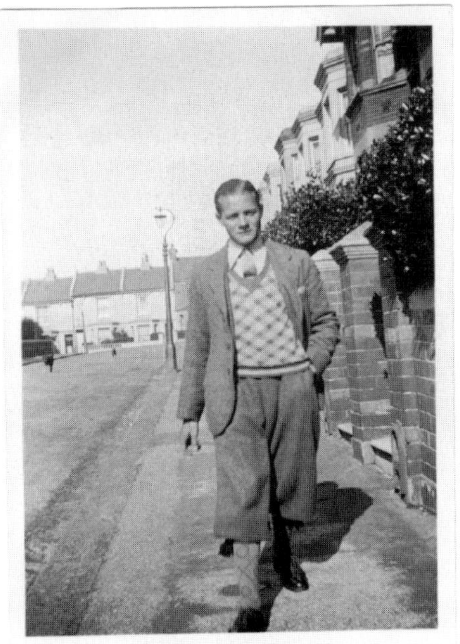

Figure 22: Roll film print on chloride paper. Though introduced in the 1920s, plus-fours were still popular, and the taste for patterned pullovers and socks was undiminished when this picture was taken (probably by a Box Brownie) in 1932.

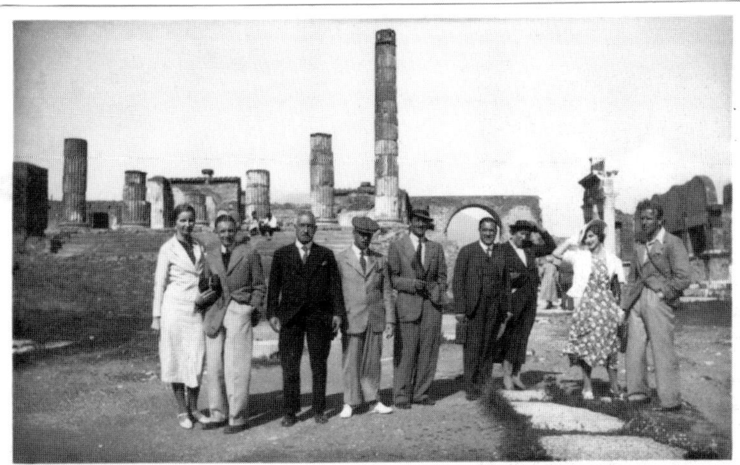

Figure 23: Postcard. Floral prints, defined waists, tilted hats (for both sexes), broad lapels, wide trouser legs and a soft collar show what the well-dressed tourist was wearing in the 1930s. Of the three cameras, one can be made out as a box and one as a folding model.

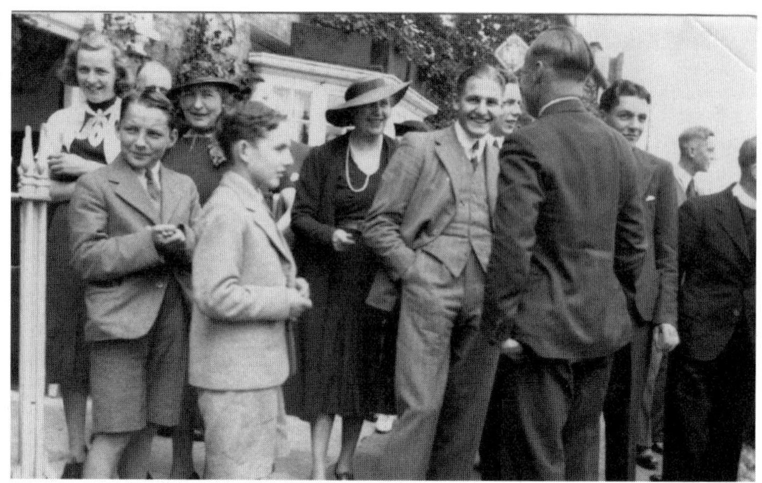

Figure 24: Postcard. Postmarked '6 Au 38', this photograph shows men with roomy trouser legs and generous lapels. Built-in soft collars (the clerical example apart) had become quite normal. Women's hats were often tilted, and skirts ended just below the knee.

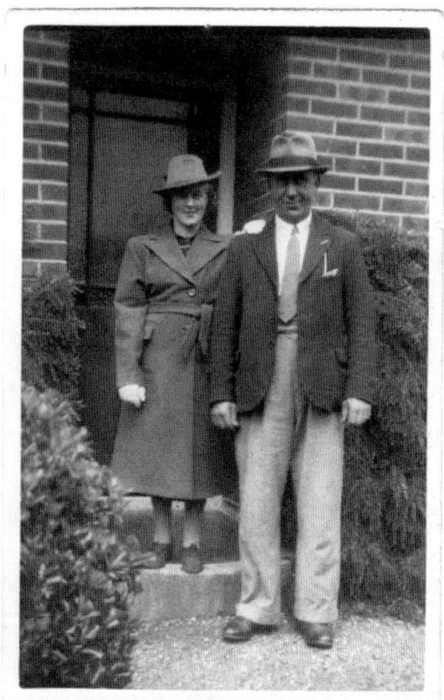

Figure 25: Postcard. Inscribed 'Mildred & George 1943', this photograph has strong echoes of the 1930s and a suggestion of clothes being required to last. Mildred wears sensible shoes; but there is a wave in her hair.

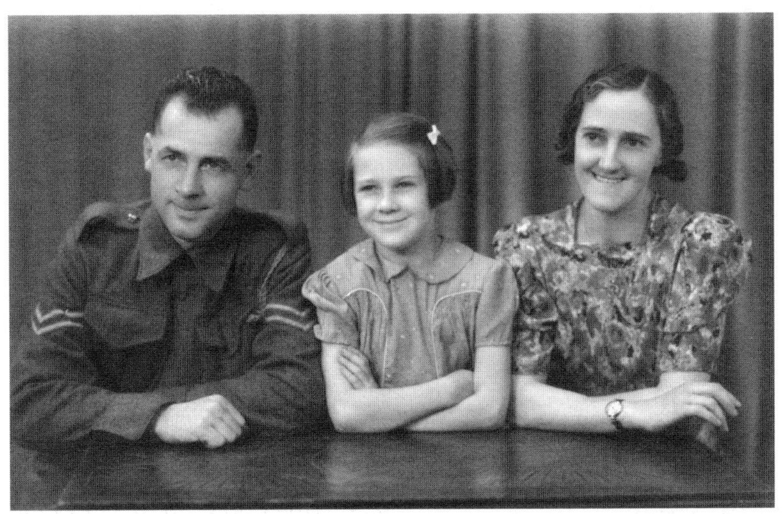

Figure 26: Postcard; Marie Podmore, Nelson. By the Second World War the battledress blouse had appeared. The mother's waved hair and floral, square-shouldered dress are typical of the 1940s. The happy mood suggests reunion rather than parting.

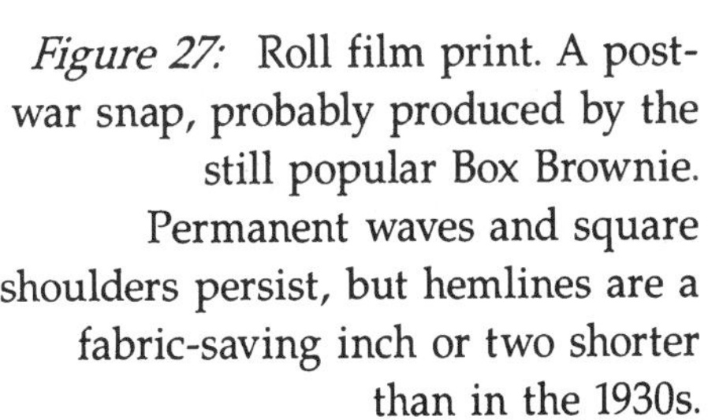

Figure 27: Roll film print. A post-war snap, probably produced by the still popular Box Brownie. Permanent waves and square shoulders persist, but hemlines are a fabric-saving inch or two shorter than in the 1930s.

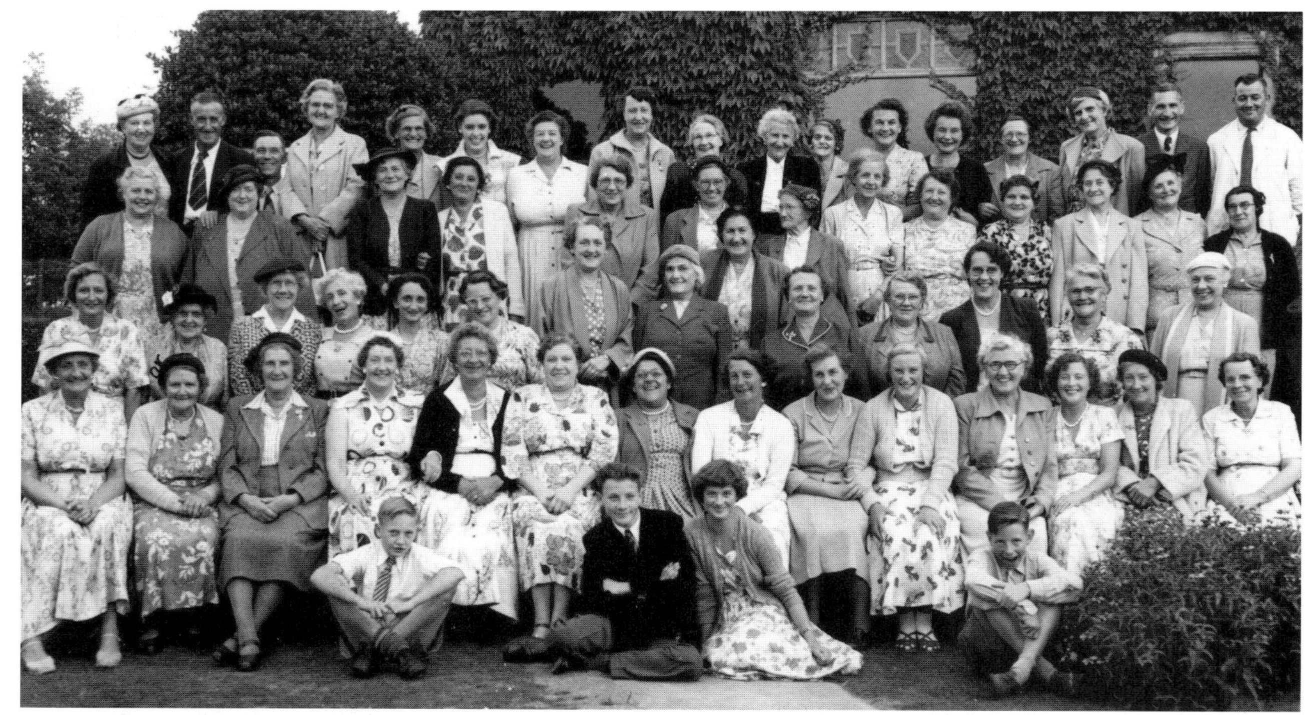

Figure 28: Print. A British Legion Women's Section outing. Beltless coats, bare heads, cardigans, and floral prints with large designs (which waste more fabric in the making up) all show that, even amongst conservative dressers, the 1950s have arrived.

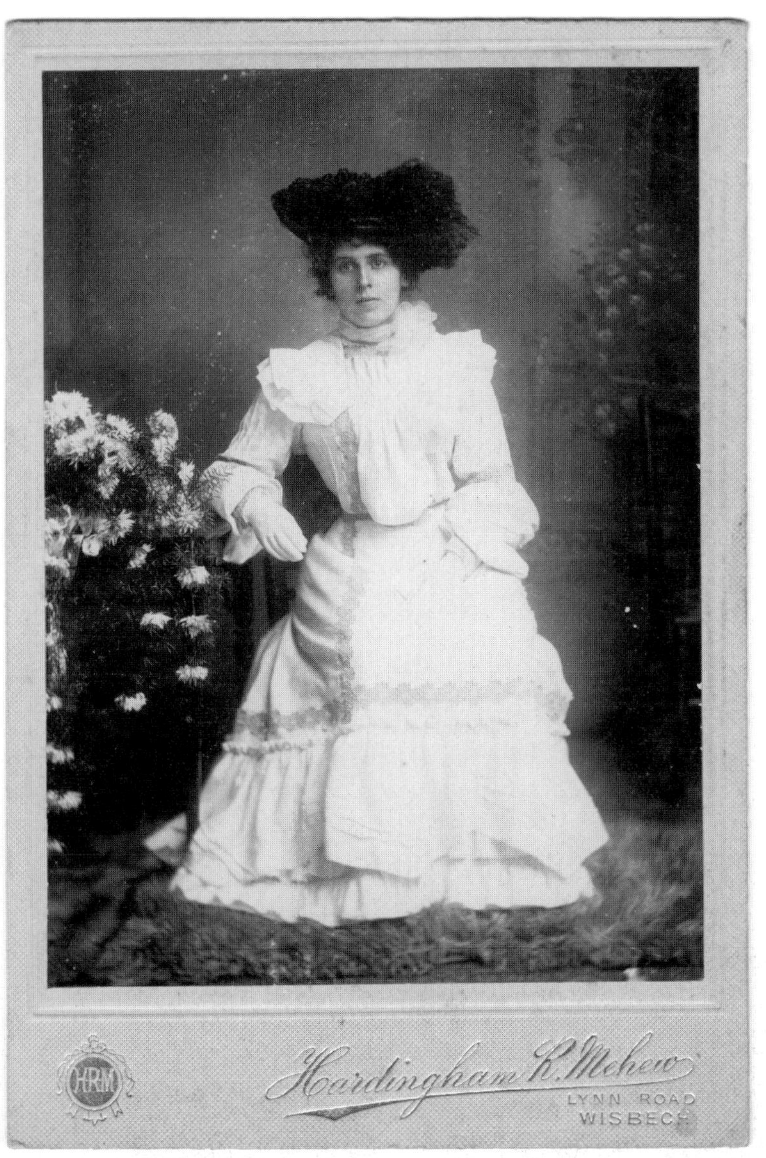

Figure 29: Cabinet print; Hardingham R Mehew, Wisbech. Directories and fashion combine to suggest a date of about 1904-8. Whilst the wedding dress with veil was growing in popularity, 'Sunday best' (plus big hat and flowers) was not at all unusual.

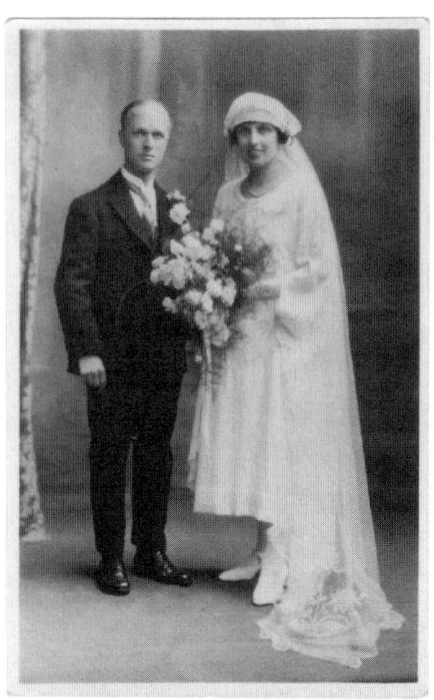

Figure 30: Postcard. When Lorna and Wallie married in 1926, bridal hemlines had risen (though not as much as everyday hemlines). The brow-hugging line of the headdress and the emphasis on the neck are characteristic of the period.

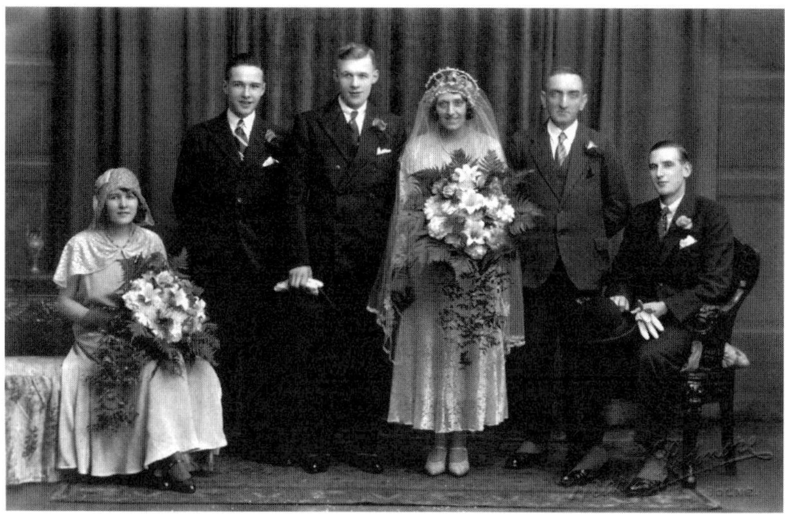

Figure 31: Postcard; Marie Podmore, Colne. Hemlines have started to drop again, the bride's headdress is set higher, the bridesmaid's cape focuses attention on the shoulders, there is a hint of mediaevalism, and spats are popular. The 1930s have arrived.

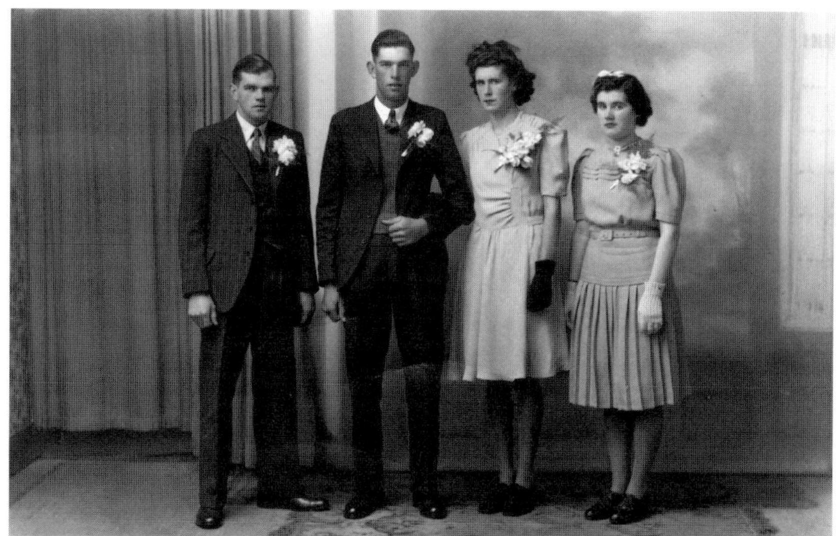

Figure 32: Postcard. Margaret marries Herbert, June 1943. This is a wartime wedding and the women's shoulders, hemlines and sensible shoes are firmly of the period. The gloves and the pullover seem in keeping with an age of austerity.

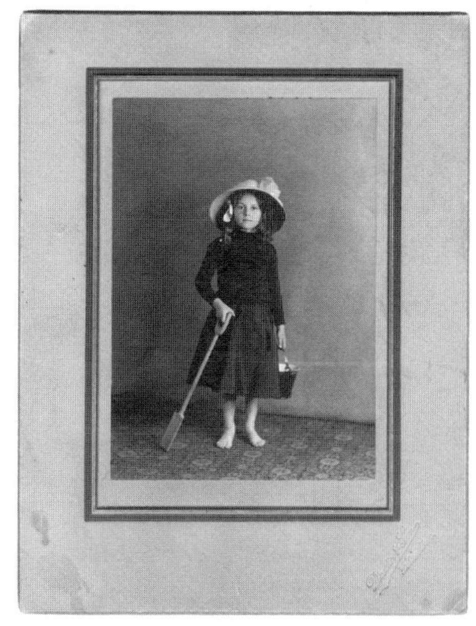

Figure 33: Mounted print; Dexter & Sons, Felixstowe. 'Enid at Felixstowe 1907 aged 5 years'. A studio visit was still the way to commemorate a trip to the seaside, and the sun was still (as it has since become again) something to be protected from.

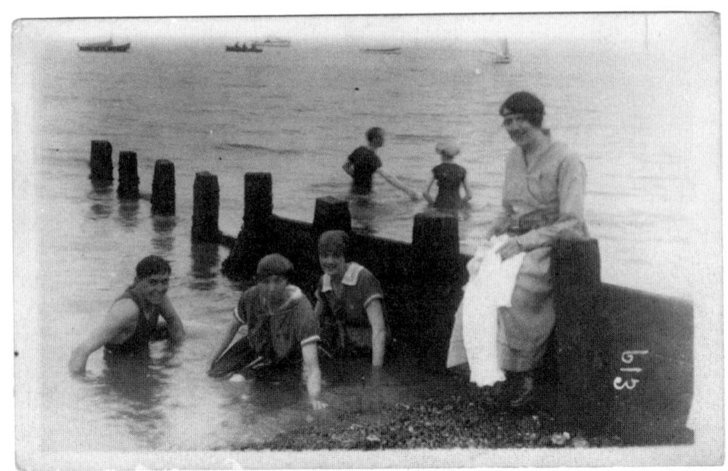

Figure 34: Postcard. 'Whitstable 1919'. The women wear two-piece costumes, with slightly nautical trim, and bathing hats. The costume of the man in the foreground seems quite advanced. The sleeved version in the background was still more customary.

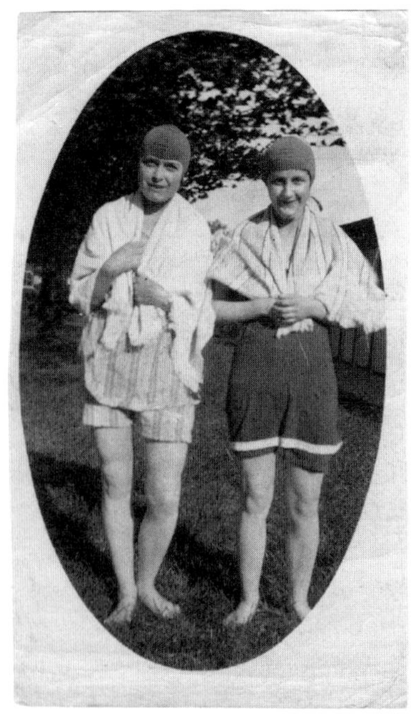

Figure 35: Roll film print. This seems to date from the 1920s. Both one- and two-piece garments are on display. They have short legs and are probably sleeveless. Rubber bathing caps grew in popularity during the decade.

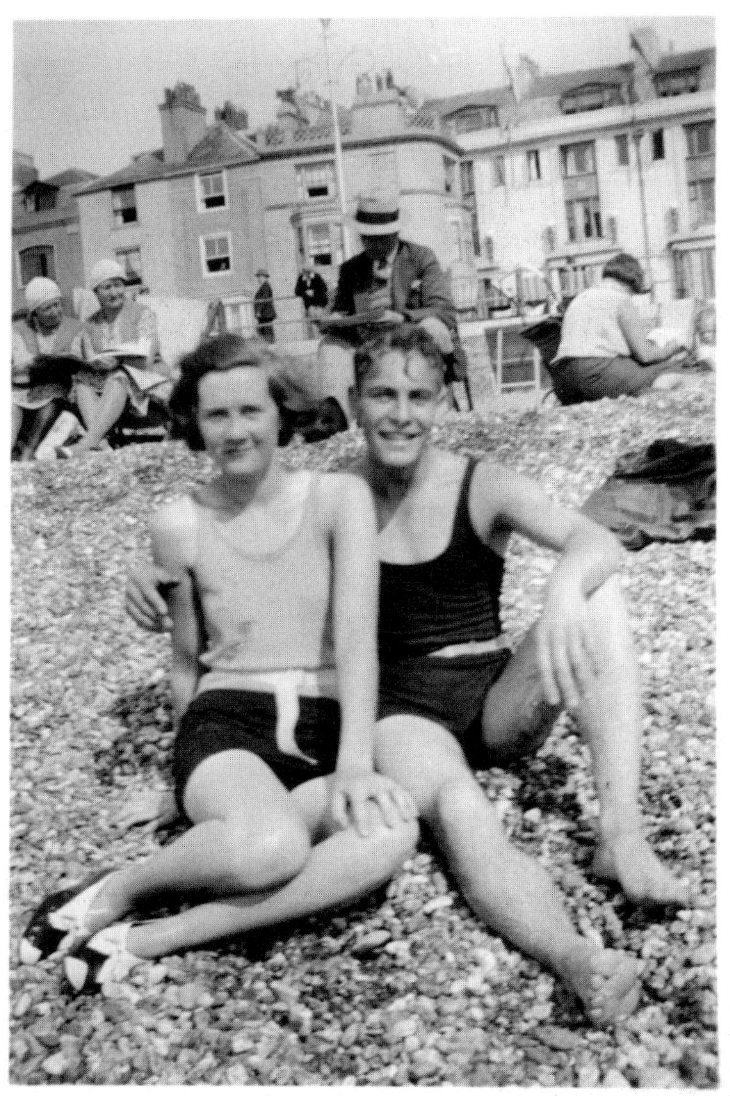

Figure 36: Roll film print. A 1932 Box Brownie snap on Velox paper. Limbs are now fully exposed to the sun and the girl is bareheaded. But the clothing of their elders, in the background, makes little or no concession to the holiday setting.

Processes

(Note: Processes shown as pre-1910 were in use throughout the Edwardian period)

10	15	20	25	30	35	40	45	50	55	60	65

<------------------(- - - - - - - -)   ----
platinum prints   sepia, deckle-edged Polaroids

<--- - - - - - -   ------------------------------------->
carbon prints (including autotype process)   Polaroid images 2⅛x3¾ inches

<-------------- - - - - -   ------------------------------------->
tintypes   black & white Polaroids

<----------------------   ------
opal prints   very faded black & white Polaroids

<--- - - - - -
chloride developing-out paper (gaslight paper/Velox)

<- - - - - - - - --
chloro-bromide developing-out paper

<--- - - - - -   -------------------->
printing-out paper   Polaroid images 2⅛x2⅞ inches

                            ------
coloured Polaroids on mounting cards, or curled (until c1966)

<------------------- -
glass negatives

<----------------------------------- - - - - - - - - - - - - - - - - -
nitro-cellulose negatives

              -------------------------------------->
safety film negatives

----
autographic film

10	15	20	25	30	35	40	45	50	55	60	65

Additional later dates:

resin–coated printing paper from c1970   'black patch' Polaroids from 1972

DATING CHART 2

Formats

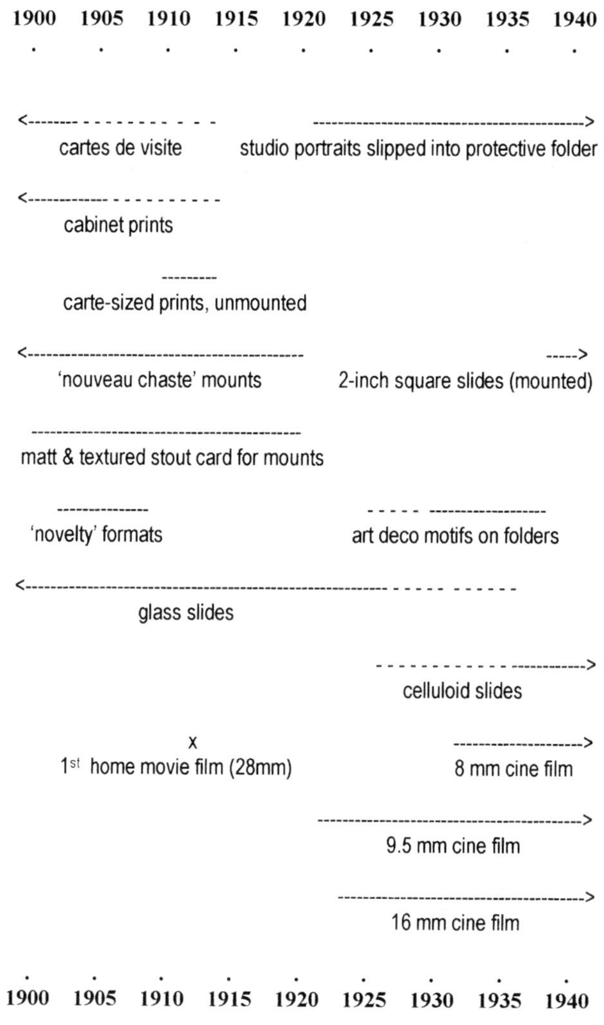

1900 1905 1910 1915 1920 1925 1930 1935 1940

<---------- - - - - - - - - - -   --->
    cartes de visite   studio portraits slipped into protective folder

<-------------- - - - - - - - - -
    cabinet prints

    ----
    carte-sized prints, unmounted

<--   ----->
    'nouveau chaste' mounts   2-inch square slides (mounted)

----
matt & textured stout card for mounts

    ----------------   - - - - - ------------------
    'novelty' formats   art deco motifs on folders

<-- - - - - - - - - - -
    glass slides

- - - - - - - - - - - - - ------------>
    celluloid slides

    X   ----------------------->
1st home movie film (28mm)   8 mm cine film

-->
9.5 mm cine film

-->
16 mm cine film

1900 1905 1910 1915 1920 1925 1930 1935 1940

(For postcards, see separate chart)

Postcards

```
    1900   1905   1910   1915   1920   1925   1930   1935   1940
      .      .      .      .      .      .      .      .      .

      <-------------------------------------------------
                      various sizes
                                          ------------------------------->
                                          sizes within range 2¾-4 x 4⅛-5⅛ inches

      <----  ------------------------------------------------------------->
      undivided back       no mention of postal regulations

          ---------
      'inland postage only' + 'may now be used'

            --------      ------------------------------------------------->
      'inland postage only; no 'now'    portraits unlikely to have passed through the post

            --------
      reference to fairly complex postal regulations

          ------------------                                    --
              Edward VII                                    Edward VIII

      <--   ------------------------------------------  ------------>
      Victoria                    George V                    George VI

          ------------------------------------   ----
                  ½d post                1½d post

                              -----   ------------------------------------->
                              1d post              1d post

          --    ---------------
      blue ½d stamp  yellow-green ½d stamp

          --------      ------------------------------------------------->
          blue-green ½d stamp              green ½d stamp

      <-----------------    -----      -------
          undivided back (US)   2c postage (US)  2c postage (US)

      <------------------------------
          white border unusual (US)
      .      .      .      .      .      .      .      .      .
    1900   1905   1910   1915   1920   1925   1930   1935   1940
```

Colour and Light

```
   15     20     25     30     35     40     45     50     55     60     65     70
   .      .      .      .      .      .      .      .      .      .      .      .

<------------------------------------ - - - -                        - - - - - - - --->
        (from 1907) Autochrome                              studio portraits in colour

                                                 ------------------------------------->
                                                        Kodacolor  (in UK)

                                                    --------------------------------->
                                                        Kodak Ektachrome (in UK)

                                     X              --------------------------------->
                              Dufaycolor introduced       Agfacolor (in UK)

                          -------------------------      ------------------------->
                                rather muted colour       35mm Kodacolor & Fujicolor

                                          ---------------------- - - -
                                                over-bright colour

<--------------------------------------------------------------------- - - - - - - -
              studio portraits generally monochrome

                                                            ---------------->
                                                              Instamatic colour

                                     X                      ---------------->
                          Sakura & Ansco colour introduced   Polaroid colour

                                          X              ------------------->
                                 Ferraniacolor introduced   colour slides

      - - - - - - - - - - - - - - - - - - - - - ------------------------------------->
                                flash photographs

                                          - - - - - - --------------------------->
                                black & white indoor pictures without flash

                                          --------------------------------->
                                                Ilfochrome slides

   .      .      .      .      .      .      .      .      .      .      .      .
   15     20     25     30     35     40     45     50     55     60     65     70
```

Roll Film Negative Sizes

(The longer dimension is given first, regardless of whether an image is in portrait or landscape format. The time span may cover more than one brand or serial number of film.)

Inches	Centimetres	Introduced	Production ended	Notes
7x5	c17.8x12.7	1898	1949	
6½x4¼	c16.5x10.8	1906	??	still in production 1908
5½x3¼	c13.9x8.3	1903	1971	
5x4	c12.7x10.2	1896	1949	
4⅞x2⅞	c12.4x7.3	1916	1971	
4¼x3¼	c10.8x8.3	1900	1961	
4¼x2½	c10.8x6.4	1899	1984	
3½x3½	c8.9x8.9	1895	1956	
3¼x2¼	c8.3x5.7	1897		produced throughout century
3x2	c7.6x5.1	1912	1951	
2½x1⅝	c6.4x4.1 *	1902	1995	
2¼x2¼	c5.7x5.7	1900	1949	
2¼x1¼	c5.7x3.2	during 1930s	??	
2x1½	c5.1x3.8	1895	1933	
1¾x1⅜	c4.4x3.5	1934	??	
c1¾x1¼	4.4x3.2	1916	??	
c1⅝x1⅛	4x2.8 *	1935	1985	
1½x1¼	c3.8x3.2	during 1930s	??	
c1⅜x⅞	3.5x2.4	mid-1920s	continues	= 35mm; developed 1914; marketed 1920s; popular from mid-1930s
c1⅛x1⅛	2.8x2.8	1963	1999	for Instamatic 50 & 100
c¾x½	1.9x1.3	1972	??	for Pocket Instamatic
c¾x½	1.8x1.3	during 1930s	??	
c⅜x⅜ *	1.1x0.8	1937	??	

(Where metric measurements are approximate, imperial measurements were used at the time of the film's introduction. Where approximate imperial measurements are given, the original measurements were metric. Two apparent contradictions in the table [*] arise from the fact that imperial approximations are to the nearest ⅛ inch.)

Themes and Conventions

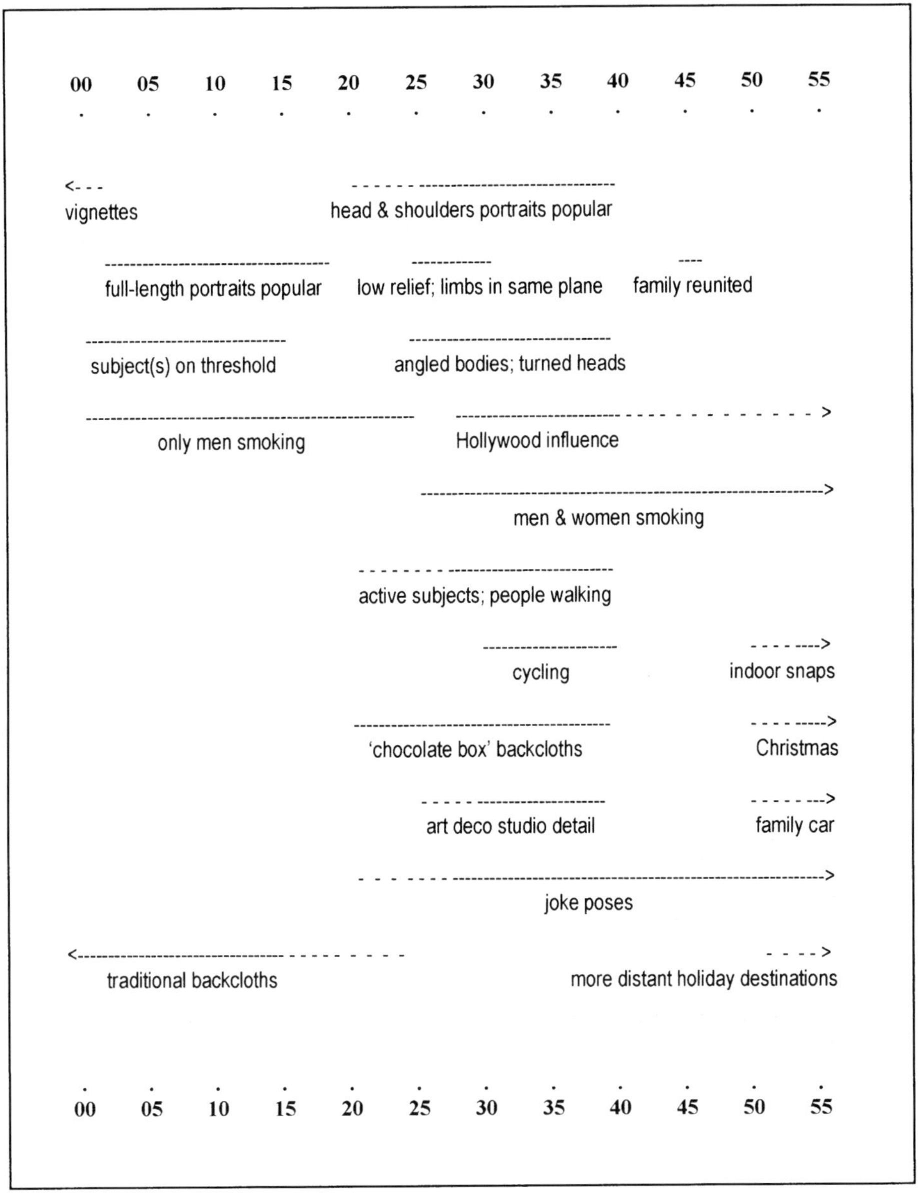

```
00    05    10    15    20    25    30    35    40    45    50    55
 .     .     .     .     .     .     .     .     .     .     .     .
```

<--- - - - - - - - ------------------------------------
vignettes   head & shoulders portraits popular

------------------------------   ------------   ----
full-length portraits popular   low relief; limbs in same plane   family reunited

----------------------------------   --------------------------------
subject(s) on threshold   angled bodies; turned heads

--   --------------------------- - - - - - - - - - - >
only men smoking   Hollywood influence

                    -->
                    men & women smoking

                    - - - - - - --------------------------------
                    active subjects; people walking

                              --------------------   - - - - ---->
                              cycling   indoor snaps

                    ------------------------------------   - - - - ---->
                    'chocolate box' backcloths   Christmas

                              - - - - -------------------   - - - - --->
                              art deco studio detail   family car

                    - - - - - - - -->
                    joke poses

<----------------------------------- - - - - - - -   - - - ->
traditional backcloths   more distant holiday destinations

```
00    05    10    15    20    25    30    35    40    45    50    55
 .     .     .     .     .     .     .     .     .     .     .     .
```

Outdoor Settings

```
    05    10    15    20    25    30    35    40    45    50    55    60
     .     .     .     .     .     .     .     .     .     .     .     .

- - - --------------------------                      ---------------------------->
  non-church background for wedding groups               all-standing wedding groups

                        ---------------------------------------------------------->
                                   wedding groups outside church

- - - - ---------------------- - - - - - - - - - - - - -      -------------------->
       wedding groups posed on more than one level                brighter bicycles

                          --------------------------------------------------------->
                                      white lines on roads

                            ------------------------------------------------------->
                                         traffic lights

                              ----------------------------------------------------->
                                        Belisha beacons

      ---------------------- - - - - -                       - - - -  ------------->
               T-model Ford                            round-nosed cars, 2CV & 'Beetle'

                              ----------------------------------------------------->
                                           L plates

                          --------------------------------------------------------->
                                     roofed London buses

                              ----------------------- - - - - - - -
                                         trolley buses

                                ---------------- - - - - -              --->
                                       beach defences                   Minis

  ---------------------        - - - - - - ------------------------------------------>
    seaside beach-vendors      developed seaside promenades, including vendors

                                      -------- - - - - - --------      ----------->
                                       classless holiday camps          estate cars

  ---------------------                                       --------------------->
   uncluttered seaside promenades                              working-class camps

     .     .     .     .     .     .     .     .     .     .     .     .
    05    10    15    20    25    30    35    40    45    50    55    60
```

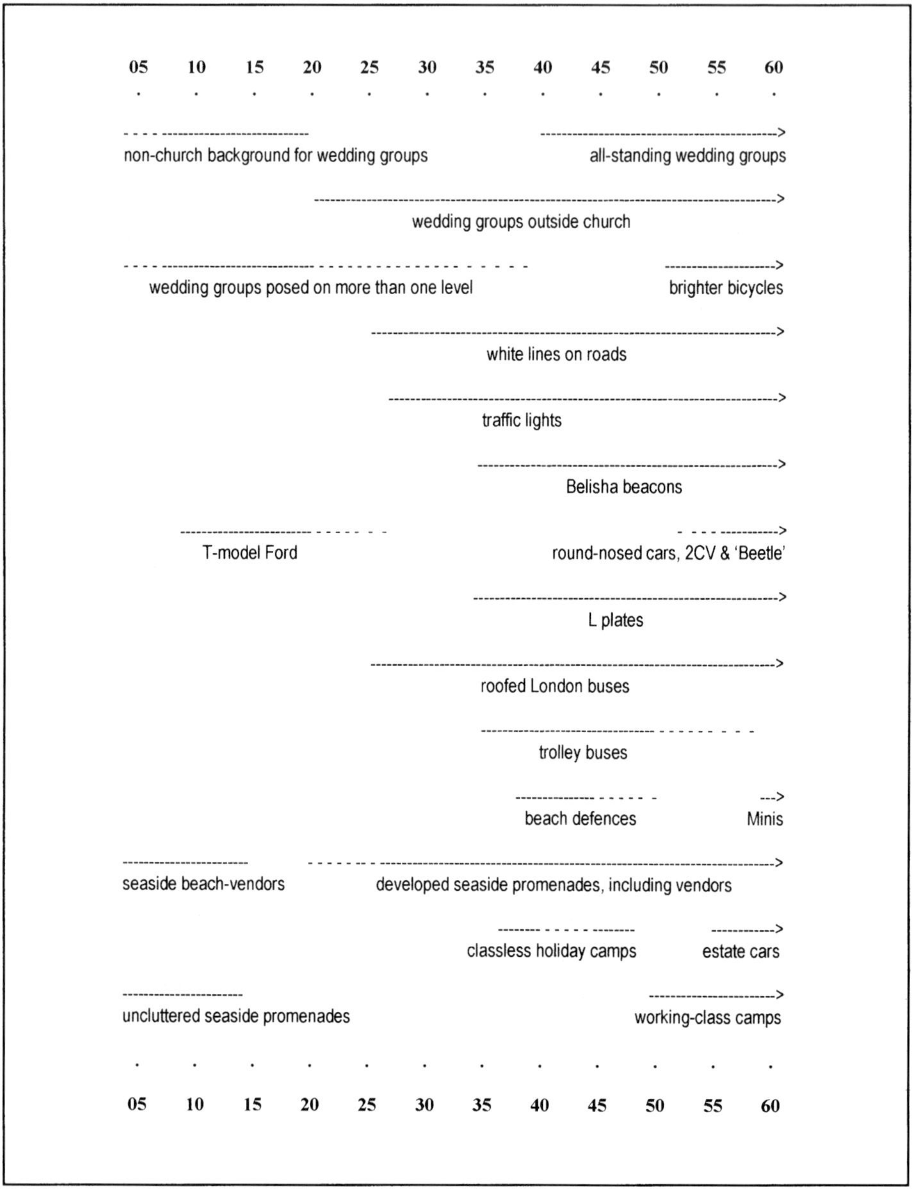

Vehicle Registration

Structure of registration number:

Sequence	Example	Registered
Letter, number, letter	A 1 B	1883-1904
1 or 2 letters, up to 4 figures	AB 1234	1904-1933
3 letters, up to 3 figures	ABC 123	1933-1953
up to 3 figures, 3 letters	123 ABC	1953-1965
3 letters, up to 3 figures, suffix letter	ABC 123 A	1963-1983
prefix letter, up to 3 figures, 3 letters	A 123 ABC	1983-2001

Suffix and prefix letters:

(For the sake of completeness, and to help those dating their own pictures, the full list is given.)

Suffix	Introduced	Prefix	Introduced
A	Jan 1963	A	Aug 1983
B	Jan 1964	B	Aug 1984
C	Jan 1965	C	Aug 1985
D	Jan 1966	D	Aug 1986
E	Jan 1967	E	Aug 1987
F	Aug 1967	F	Aug 1988
G	Aug 1968	G	Aug 1989
H	Aug 1969	H	Aug 1990
J	Aug 1970	J	Aug 1991
K	Aug 1971	K	Aug 1992
L	Aug 1972	L	Aug 1993
M	Aug 1973	M	Aug 1994
N	Aug 1974	N	Aug 1995
P	Aug 1975	P	Aug 1996
R	Aug 1976	R	Aug 1997
S	Aug 1977	S	Aug 1998
T	Aug 1978	T	Mar 1999
V	Aug 1979	V	Sep 1999
W	Aug 1980	W	Mar 2000
X	Aug 1981	X	Sep 2000
Y	Aug 1982	Y	Mar 2001

Women's Clothes 1: Bodice, Sleeves and Skirts

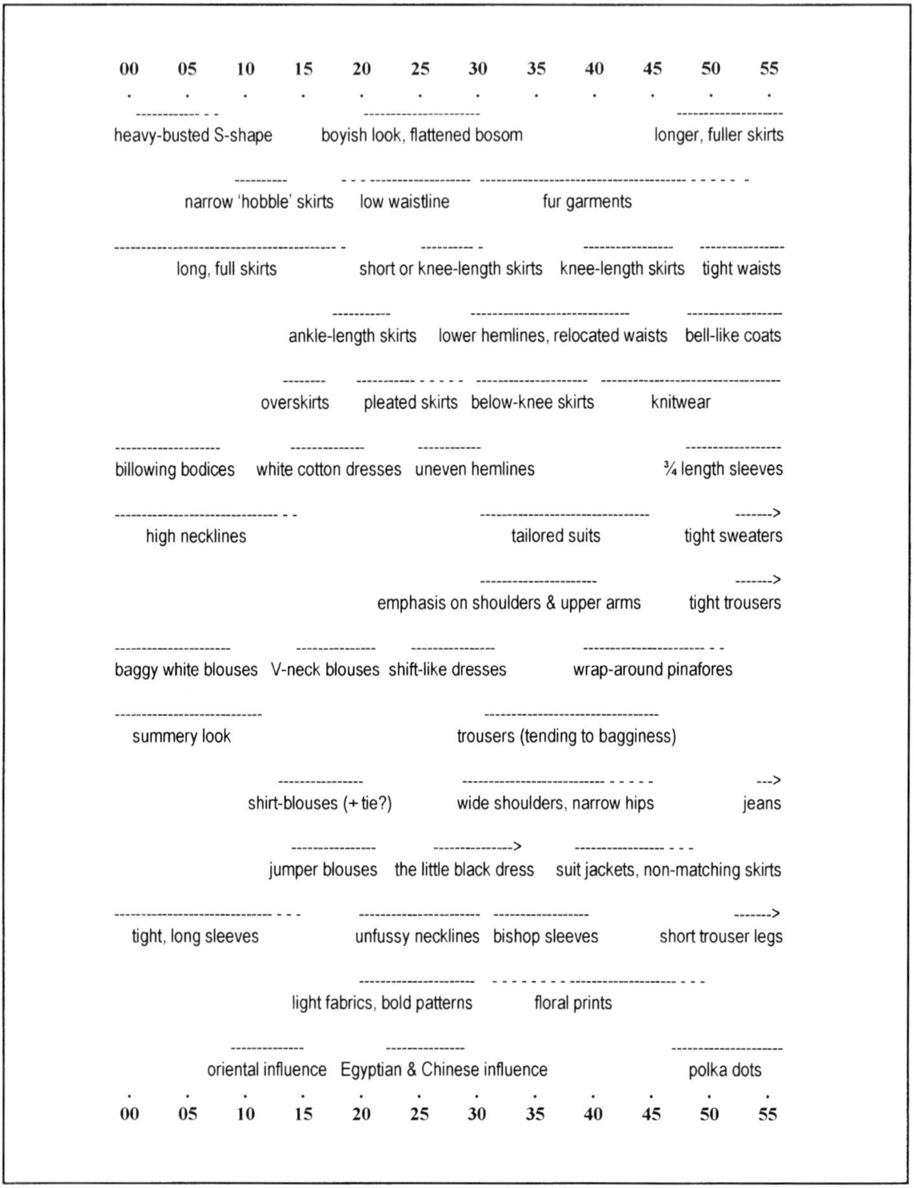

```
     00    05    10    15    20    25    30    35    40    45    50    55
      .     .     .     .     .     .     .     .     .     .     .     .
   ------------ - -              ------------------              --------------------
   heavy-busted S-shape        boyish look, flattened bosom       longer, fuller skirts

            ----------    - - --------------- ------------------------------------ - - - - -
            narrow 'hobble' skirts   low waistline            fur garments

   ----------------------------------------- -      ---------- -     ------------------   ----------------
            long, full skirts              short or knee-length skirts  knee-length skirts  tight waists

                       ----------    ------------------------------   ------------------
                       ankle-length skirts  lower hemlines, relocated waists  bell-like coats

                       --------  ----------- - - - -  -------------------  --------------------------------
                       overskirts    pleated skirts  below-knee skirts    knitwear

   -------------------        --------------     -----------                  ------------------
   billowing bodices   white cotton dresses  uneven hemlines                 ¾ length sleeves

   ----------------------------- - -                  ------------------------------      ------->
         high necklines                               tailored suits                  tight sweaters

                                                  ----------------------      ------->
                                              emphasis on shoulders & upper arms     tight trousers

   ----------------------    --------------    ----------------    ----------------------- - -
   baggy white blouses   V-neck blouses  shift-like dresses     wrap-around pinafores

   -------------------------               -----------------------------------
         summery look                         trousers (tending to bagginess)

                    ----------------        ------------------------- - - - - -        --->
                    shirt-blouses (+ tie?)    wide shoulders, narrow hips           jeans

                    ----------------   -------------->   ------------------ - - -
                    jumper blouses   the little black dress  suit jackets, non-matching skirts

   ------------------------------- - - -     ----------------------  ------------------       ------->
        tight, long sleeves                  unfussy necklines   bishop sleeves       short trouser legs

                         ----------------------   - - - - - - ------------------------ - - -
                    light fabrics, bold patterns     floral prints

                         --------------     ----------------                   --------------------
                    oriental influence  Egyptian & Chinese influence            polka dots
      .     .     .     .     .     .     .     .     .     .     .     .
     00    05    10    15    20    25    30    35    40    45    50    55
```

Womens' Clothes 2: Hats, Hair and Accessories

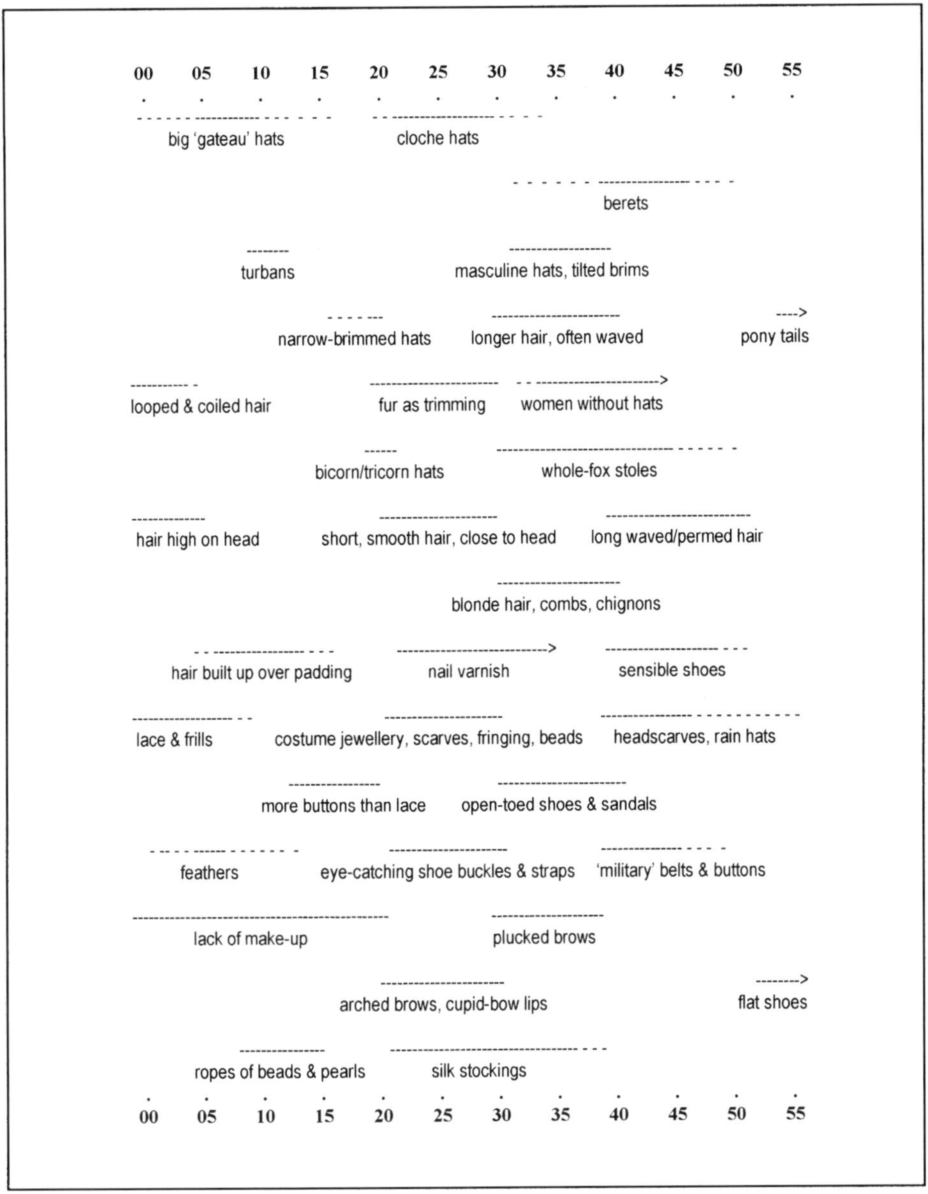

```
00    05    10    15    20    25    30    35    40    45    50    55
 .     .     .     .     .     .     .     .     .     .     .     .

- - - - - ------------ - - - - - -      - - ---------------- - - - -
      big 'gateau' hats                     cloche hats


                              - - - - - - ---------------- - - - -
                                            berets


              --------                ------------------
              turbans                 masculine hats, tilted brims


                          - - - - ---      ------------------          ---->
              narrow-brimmed hats   longer hair, often waved        pony tails


 ----------- -            --------------------  - - ------------------->
 looped & coiled hair       fur as trimming    women without hats


                          ------             ---------------------- - - - - -
              bicorn/tricorn hats             whole-fox stoles


 --------------           ----------------------       ---------------------------
 hair high on head        short, smooth hair, close to head   long waved/permed hair


                                     -----------------------
                          blonde hair, combs, chignons


      - - ---------------- - - -     ----------------------->     ------------------- - - -
      hair built up over padding     nail varnish                 sensible shoes


 ------------------ - -           ----------------------      ----------------------------- - -
 lace & frills        costume jewellery, scarves, fringing, beads    headscarves, rain hats


              ------------------            ----------------------
              more buttons than lace        open-toed shoes & sandals


 - -- - ------- - - - - - -       ----------------------      ----------------- - - - -
      feathers                   eye-catching shoe buckles & straps   'military' belts & buttons


 -------------------------------------        --------------------
      lack of make-up                         plucked brows


                          ------------------------               -------->
              arched brows, cupid-bow lips                       flat shoes


              ----------------       ------------------------------- - - -
      ropes of beads & pearls        silk stockings
 .     .     .     .     .     .     .     .     .     .     .     .
00    05    10    15    20    25    30    35    40    45    50    55
```

Men's Clothes

```
  00    05    10    15    20    25    30    35    40    45    50    55
  ·     ·     ·     ·     ·     ·     ·     ·     ·     ·     ·     ·

------------------------- - - - - - -        - - - - - - - - ---------------------------------------------- - - - -
still some top hats                                      trilbies

------------------------------------------------- - - - ->  -----------------------------------------------------  - - - - -
          homburg hats                                   working-class flat caps

                           ----------------------              - - - - - ----->
                           double-breasted jackets             duffle coats, windcheaters

                              ----------------------                       -->
                    short jackets, padded shoulders, wide lapels       'Edwardian' look

----------------------- - - - - -              -----------                        --------->
occasional frock coats              double-breasted waistcoats               roll-neck sweaters

                                  ----------------------------------------------------- - - -
                                              Fair Isle pullovers

---------------- - - - - - - - - -     - - - ------------------------------------------------------->
high starched shirt collars                           open-necked shirts

                           ------------ - - -/--------------------
                           Oxford bags / wide trouser legs

---------------------------------      --------------------- - - -                          --->
        few turn-ups                         plus-fours                                    jeans

                           -------------------------------
                                  two-tone shoes

                    --------------             -------------
                military tunics, puttees,   military  battledress blouses,
                     peaked caps               gaiters, berets, forage caps

  ·     ·     ·     ·     ·     ·     ·     ·     ·     ·     ·     ·
  00    05    10    15    20    25    30    35    40    45    50    55
```

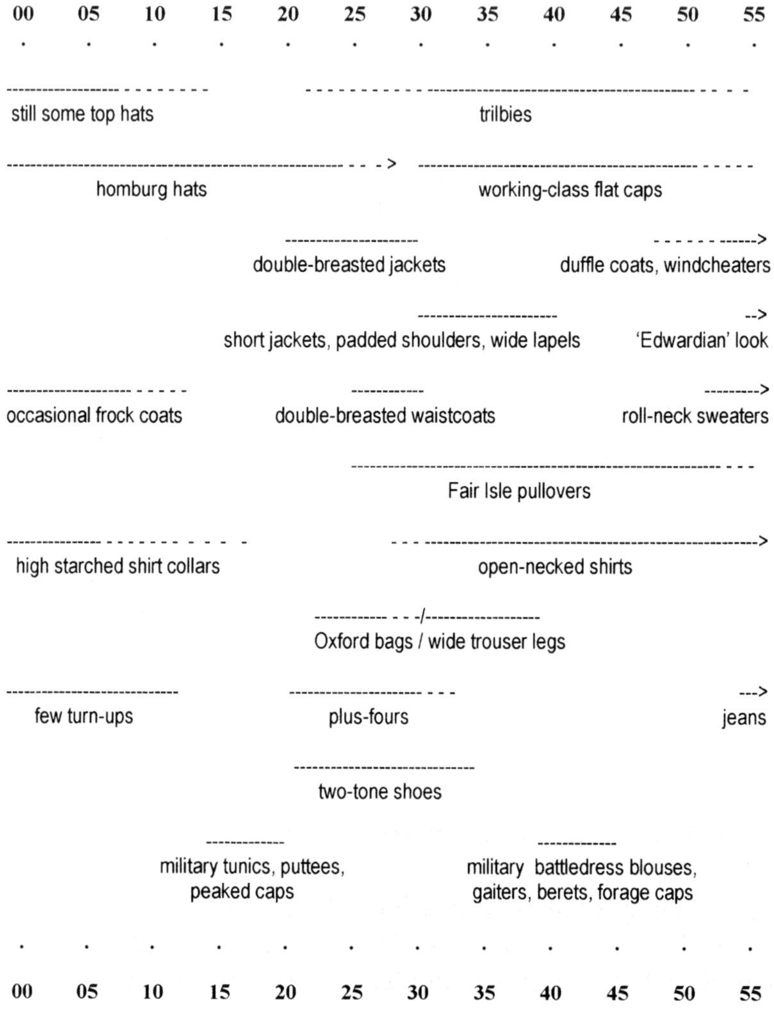

(For later fashions, the reader is referred to the lists in the text)

Bibliography

Popular photography

B. Coe and P. Gates, *The Snapshot Photograph: The Rise of Popular Photography, 1888-1939* (Ash & Grant, 1977)

C. Ford (ed.), *The Story of Popular Photography* (Century, in association with the National Museum of Photography, Film and Television, 1989)

D. Kenyon, *Inside Amateur Photography* (Batsford, 1992)

M. Langford, *Story of Photography,* 2nd edn (Focal Press, 1997)

R. Pols, *Family Photographs 1860-1945* (Public Record Office, 2002)

D. Steel and L. Taylor, *Family History in Focus* (Lutterworth Press, 1984)

Costume

A. Lansdell, *Everyday Fashions of the 20th Century* (Shire, 1999)

A. Lansdell, *Seaside Fashions 1860-1839* (Shire, 1990)

A. Lansdell, *Wedding Fashions 1860-1980*, 2nd edn (Shire, 1986)

J. Peacock, *Fashion Sourcebooks: The 1920s* (Thames & Hudson, 1997)

J. Peacock, *Fashion Sourcebooks: The 1930s* (Thames & Hudson, 1997)

J. Peacock, *Fashion Sourcebooks: The 1940s* (Thames & Hudson, 1998)

J. Peacock, *Fashion Sourcebooks: The 1950s* (Thames & Hudson, 1997)

J. Peacock, *Fashion Sourcebooks: The 1960s* (Thames & Hudson, 1998)

H. Worsley, *The Hulton Getty Picture Collection: Decades of Fashion* (Könemann, 2000)

Street scenes

C. Ayton, *A-Z Guide to British Motorcycles from the 1930s to the 1970s* (Bay View Books, 1991)

S. Beeley, *A History of Bicycles* (Studio Editions, 1992)

N. Baldwin, *A-Z of Cars of the 1920s* (Bay View Books, 1994)

M. Sedgwick and M. Gillies, *A-Z of Cars of the 1930s* (Bay View Books, 1989)

M. Sedgwick and M. Gillies, *A-Z of Cars: 1945-1970,* 2nd edn (Bay View Books, 1989)

K. Turner, *The Directory of British Tramways* (Patrick Stephens, 1996)